BECOMING A FATHER
How to nurture and enjoy your family

Matthew may not remember these times as he grows older,
but I will never forget.

THE GROWING FAMILY SERIES

BECOMING A FATHER

How to Nurture and Enjoy Your Family

William Sears, M.D.

La Leche League International
Schaumburg, Illinois

December 1986
©1986 by William Sears, M.D.
All rights reserved
Fourth printing, August 1998

Printed in the United States of America
Photo credits:
    cover, Martha Sears
    p. 8, 55, Dale Pfeiffer
    p. 183, Anne Engelhardt
    p. 193, Colleen Weiland
    p. 197, 204, ©Richard Ebbitt
    others, William Sears
        Martha Sears
Illustrations by John Seid and Ed Ryborz
Book and cover design by Lucy Lesiak
Library of Congress Card Catalog Number 86-083064
ISBN 0-912500-21-2

Dedicated to my children who taught me how to become a father—once I learned how to listen to them—Jim, Bob, Peter, Hayden, Erin, and Matthew

CONTENTS

Foreword   xi

Chapter 1
Father to Father   1

   *True Confessions • My New Role • Attachment Fathering •
   Father-Baby Addiction • As a Father Grows*

Chapter 2
Fathering before Birth   15
   *Caring for Your Baby before Birth • Father Talks, Baby Listens •
   Father Feelings during Pregnancy • Understanding Changes in
   Your Wife • Fears and Facts about the Future*

Chapter 3
Fathering Your Newborn   25

Fathers and Birth • Is Too Much Expected of Dad? • The Bonding Triangle: Father-Mother-Baby Attachment • Postpartum Depression • Taking Care of the Baby

Chapter 4
The Breastfeeding Father   51

What Every Father Needs to Know about Breastfeeding • Advantages of Breastfeeding • Weaning—a Time of Fulfillment • Should Father Give Baby a Bottle?

Chapter 5
Understanding and Enjoying Your
Baby's Development   67

Birth to Three Months • Three to Six Months • Six to Nine Months • Nine to Twelve Months

Chapter 6
Nighttime Fathering   109

How Babies Sleep • Where Should Babies Sleep? • Fathering to Sleep

Chapter 7
Is There Sex after Childbirth?   119

Why Your Sex Life Isn't the Same • Rekindling the Sexual Fire • For Mothers Only • Maturing as a Father—Maturing as a Man

Chapter 8
Fathering the High Need Child   131

Recognizing the High Need Baby • Understanding High Need Babies and Their Mothers • Fathering the High Need Child • Preventing Mother Burnout • Recognizing the Early Signs of Burnout • What's in It for Dads

Chapter 9
Solo Fathering   147

Father as a Baby-Sitter • Fathers and the Working Mother •
What Can Fathers Do?

Chapter 10
Where's Dad?   161

Attachment Fathering and Separation • A Smooth Re-entry •
Tips to Lessen the Effects of Separation • The Absent Father

Chapter 11
Father's Role in Discipline   169

Discipline Begins at Birth • Disciplining Your Toddler • Father's
Role in Setting Limits • Corrective Discipline

Chapter 12
Father as a Role Model   191

Father as Nurturer • Comforter • Decision-Maker • Model of
Emotional Expression • Modeling Priorities • Values • Trust •
Developing Sexual Identity • Masculinity • Femininity • Some
Thoughts on Homosexuality • Modeling the Marriage
Relationship

Chapter 13
Fathering the Older Child   211

Fathering the One- to Three-Year-Old • Build Positive Memories •
Father Fun • Fathering the Three- to Six-Year-Old • Fathering
Your Child from Six to Ten • Father's Role during the Teenage
Years • Influence, Not Control

Chapter 14
A Closing Story   235

Index   239

FOREWORD

"Experience is a great teacher; a fool will learn from no other." *Poor Richard's Almanack*

Some of us have to learn the "hard way," to paraphrase Ben Franklin, instead of learning from the advice of others. Parents are no exception, learning much about their roles by trial and error. We regret our errors because "parenting is inherently a guilt-producing profession," as Dr. William Sears reminds us.

Fathers who read this book, however, can avoid guilt by learning from Dr. Sears' mistakes, as well as from his considerable knowledge of pediatrics. The father of six, he admits it took several children before he got the hang of fatherhood. In BECOMING A FATHER, Dr. Sears provides creative ideas—consistent with La Leche League's philosophy—about becoming a competent father.

"Fathering means carrying through with what you started," says Dr. Sears. Carrying through, he explains, means being sensitive to the mother's needs so she may be a better mother. Carrying through means giving children the time and attention they need from their father. It means learning the joys of nurturing, something fathers may have more opportunity to do since more mothers are in the workforce outside the home.

The unfortunate truth, however, is that fewer fathers than ever before are carrying through with their responsibilities. The record rates of divorce and single-parent families mean that dad isn't around much, if at all, for millions of kids.

The father's relationship to his children is different from the mother's, but it is essential nonetheless. The sooner society recognizes that fact, the better.

In this well-researched but easy-to-read volume, Dr. Sears documents the importance of the distinctive paternal role. Fathers both new and experienced can learn "the easy way" from BECOMING A FATHER.

Paul D. Froehlich
Teacher and father of two
Second generation LLL parent

CHAPTER 1

Father to Father

Speaking as one father to another, let me share a secret with you: Babies are fun, kids are a joy, and fatherhood is the only profession where you're guaranteed that the more effort you put into it the more enjoyment you will get out of it. And guess what? You get to experience these joys twenty-four hours a day, from spit-up on your lapel as you go off to work in the morning to the inevitable crying at 3:00 AM (with lots of love and smiles in between).

Fatherhood can be a joy, but only if you let it. I didn't at first. As a father of six, I missed the boat with my first three, got wiser with the fourth and fifth, and really scored with the sixth. I was a slow learner, needing the experience of having six children to discover what I should have known with the first. These successes and failures prompted me to write this book and share with you a style of parenting that took me nineteen years of fathering and fifteen years of pediatric practice to learn. I want to spare you (and your child) the mistakes that I made and offer you an approach to fathering that is richly rewarding. As I have written this book I have become both painfully aware of my shortcomings and profoundly grateful for how much my children have taught me—once I learned how to listen.

True Confessions

With our first two children I was a lousy dad and an even lousier husband. In retrospect, I realize that I married before I was really mature. I was a boy, not yet ready to think like a man. Our first two children, beautiful sons, came at a time when I was climbing the ladder of professional success. I bought into a system of medical training that preached profession first and left family a distant second. I chose a profession that was dedicated to helping families thrive but my own family barely survived.

A pediatrician should know better, right? Well, I didn't. I wasn't deliberately an absentee father, but did feel that my first responsibility was to establish my career, from which my family would ultimately profit. Also, I didn't really know that father's role was all that important in the first couple of years. Mother's care seemed to be enough for young children. I had grown up without a father and somehow had managed to tune out any realization of the importance of a father's presence. I thought that my main role was to work very hard to support my growing family, and as an intern at Harvard, I could barely do that.

After five years of marriage and two children, I had achieved increasing professional success but I was still a failure as a father. (My wife, Martha, later told me, "I suspected we were in for trouble when you took a suitcase full of medical books along on our honeymoon.") You will be hearing a lot about Martha throughout this book. She contributed to the process of making me a father even as I witnessed her development as a mother. She took up the slack of my loose involvement. Then something happened that changed me from rising young physician to devoted dad. When our two oldest sons, Bobby and Jim, were two and four, I was offered a plum position as chief pediatric resident at the Hospital for Sick Children in Toronto, the largest children's hospital in the world. I thought I had the world by the tail, but I only had the tail. Instead of quickly accepting, I hesitated. I heard an inner voice saying, "Bill, stop and take inventory of where you are." I did just that and concluded that, while accepting the job might have been good for me, everything I'd done in the past five years had been good for *me*. I hadn't thought about my family. I finally realized that although I would survive if I rejected the position, my family wouldn't survive as a unit if I accepted it. My children needed me, not my degrees and resume. They wanted and needed a father to play and wrestle with them when they were happy, and to comfort them when they were sad. They needed a father's hand to tuck them in and a deeper voice to read them to sleep, not just a dutiful good-night phone call from a father who was responsible for the welfare of 850 hospitalized children and yet shook off his commitment to his own healthy family of three.

To the surprise of my colleagues and the joy of my family I declined the position at the hospital in order to take a loftier position at home. I remember well the day I walked into the office of Dr. Harry Bain, professor and chairman of the department of pediatrics at the University of Toronto, and announced my decision. In his wise way, he replied, "Bill, I understand." Once the decision was made, instead of feeling a sense of loss, I felt a tremendous sense of gain. What I had gained was my family. For the first time in my life I realized that a father cannot make decisions that benefit him alone. I had that beautiful feeling that comes from making a decision that corresponded exactly with my gut feelings. This decision had a tremendous maturing effect on me. For the first time in years, other persons seemed more important than myself.

My New Role

Instead of accepting the position as chief resident, I was content with the private practice of pediatrics and took a part-time teaching position as assistant professor of pediatrics at the University of Toronto. But how did I get back into fathering and, for that matter, being a husband? As so often happens in a house with an absentee father, Martha had become both mother and father. When a woman is required to take on this double role she may subtly or not so subtly tune out her husband. I not only had to woo back my children, I also had to woo back my wife.

Our third child, Peter, was a transitional baby. I was the one who was in transition. I was around the house a lot and semi-actively involved, but I still didn't understand that fathers could have a nurturing role in their children's lives—that was mother's job, I thought.

Three years later, our first daughter, Hayden, came along like a wave of wisdom who would change my life forever. Hayden is one of those children who extracted every ounce of energy from both her parents and can be appreciated only in hindsight. She was wired differently than our first three children. From early on I knew that she was a special child with special needs. She was constantly fussy and demanding.

Heather Hayden Sears helped make me into a father. Her high level of needs required two mothers, and I soon found that it was up to me to be one of them. She wanted to be held, nursed, and comforted constantly. Because she protested vehemently if put down, Martha and I were always playing "pass the baby." She was in our arms by day and in our bed at night. There were days when she nursed constantly. She craved skin-to-skin contact and often fell asleep on my fuzzy chest when her mother had already given out.

Babies don't come with directions. (Even if they did, Hayden's would have been written in a foreign language!) Hayden, like all babies, did have a special language of needy cries, and we had ears and hearts that listened and responded. Somehow we all managed to bring out the best in each other.

We couldn't leave her. We were like the nursery rhyme: Anywhere that Bill and Martha went, Hayden was sure to go. She snuggled against our bodies in a baby sling rather than being wheeled in a stroller. Hayden thrived during the first year, but we survived only marginally. Yet something beautifully right was happening to me. Very subtly and gradually I was changing. After a year of feeling that I had been doing nothing but giving, I realized that I had received much in return. Hayden was teaching me how to nurture.

Hayden's needs were not only intense, they also lasted longer. She weaned from the breast when she was four years old and left our bed at four-and-a-half years. During that time I continued to grow, albeit slowly, in paternal sensitivity. I became more sensitive to all of my children, and this sensitivity carried over into our marriage. Even our sex life improved. My wife became more sensitive to me as a mate. (Nothing turns a woman on more than a man who is a sensitive and caring father.)

Because Hayden was naturally closer to Martha than to me, I began to respect the phenomenon of mother-infant attachment. I didn't feel left out of the inner circle of mother and baby. I knew that somehow I was part of it, too, but in a different way.

Because I was around the house more and actively involved, our family life became more organized. I could provide a framework around which family members could grow and develop according to their potential. My previous selfishness was giving way to sensitivity. Because the sensitivity filtered down, everyone became more sensitive to one another. My investment was beginning to pay off. I was hooked on fathering.

Attachment Fathering

However, my children were not finished with me yet. We've added two more finishing touches to our family, Erin and Matthew. With each one I've invested more and more of myself and gotten more in return. I learned *that the child helps* the father grow as much as the father helps the child develop. Nothing matures a man like fathering a bunch of kids. I don't mean just conceiving babies. Fathering means carrying through with what you started.

Even with our fifth child, Erin, I didn't feel as close to her as my wife did. After all the baby comes out of the mother's body, so it seemed natural that there would be a stronger mother-child bond than father-child bond. Although I could understand that there might be some biological truth to this concept, I still didn't want to be left out. After all, half of those forty-six chromosomes in every single cell of our children came from me. My wife often described her relationship to our babies by saying, "I feel absolutely addicted to the baby." I wanted to feel "addicted," too.

While I was prepared to accept the biology behind the mother-baby relationship, I wondered if there was some further explanation for this apparent addiction? Perhaps this mysterious bonding was a byproduct of simply spending more time with the baby. Whatever it was that provided the magical glue cementing mother and baby together, I wanted some of it. Although I realized I could not manufacture the hormones that travel through a mother's internal highways and tell her which turns to take, nor could I feed the baby (mothers have an exclusive patent in that area), I was determined to become a one-hundred-percent father. I didn't want to compete with my wife's mothering, but I wanted a part of the action, too.

I'LL HELP YOU
GROW, DAD!

And so it was on Christmas Day, 1984, when I opened a tiny box that would give me one more chance. As we gathered around the Christmas tree my wife handed me a small package. I could see a special glow in her eyes. With the help of two-and-a-half-year-old Erin, the wrappings were soon gone revealing a box and a note. The box was labeled Early Pregnancy Test and the test tube inside revealed a purple ring showing positive results. The note from my wife read "God has blessed us with our sixth child."

I couldn't have been happier! I had another chance at being a real father! By this time I had resolved my conflicts about mother's role vs. father's role and I had given up my fantasy about wanting to be a mother; but I knew I wanted to be the best darn father in the whole wide world! Later that week, I heard a familiar slogan on a TV commercial— "Be all that you can be . . ." and I knew that's what I wanted to do! Be all that I could be to my unborn child and the rest of my family.

Our pregnancy was pleasantly uncomplicated. My wife could feel our baby grow; I could only watch my wife grow. What she could see *and* feel, I could only see. But I didn't feel left out at this point because I knew my role was simply to love and nurture my wife as she loved and nourished our baby.

I made a diligent effort to be understanding of Martha's physical discomforts, her mood swings, her short fuse, and her sometimes diminished interest in sex. I made sure that she got enough rest, that she knew I loved her. She felt my commitment and responded accordingly.

As we lay in bed together at night during the final three months I would watch the undulating movements of Martha's abdomen as our baby moved. Each night I would lay my hand on her abdomen, the "bulge," as I called it, and talk to our baby. I think that Matthew heard me.

All during this pregnancy I was in commitment training, learning to be all that I could be to Martha and our children, learning how to give, yet expecting no immediate returns for myself.

Near the end of July, I was in the middle of a well-baby exam when my nurse rushed in. "Your wife's on the phone. Her water broke and she wants you to hurry home." On the drive home I went through the usual fatherly fears and lists of "what if's." (As director of a newborn nursery I spent so much time attending high-risk deliveries that it was easy to forget that most babies are born healthy.)

Our birth attendant was at another delivery, but Martha was in control. I was marginal. As I saw the bulge of water-matted hair starting to appear in the birth canal, some get-yourself-under-control forces clicked in and I realized that I was going to be the first person to touch our baby. As his slippery little body slid into my anxious hands, I knew that we were destined for a special relationship. He breathed immediately. So did I. Instinctively, Martha reached down and gently pulled Matthew up to her breasts. As I cut the cord I felt that I was giving Matthew and Martha permission to momentarily separate and then quickly reunite, continuing their feeling of oneness in a different way.

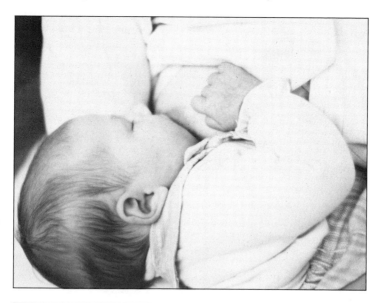

Mothers have an exclusive patent on feeding babies.

After Matthew's birth, I was supercharged. I hovered over the mother-baby pair like an eagle protecting the nest. There were to be no interferences. No one was allowed access to my wife and baby without going through me. While the jury is still out on the long-term effects of birth bonding, I wanted a special period of time set aside for mother, father, and baby to get to know each other. The older children had strict orders that this was a special period when mommy was to be given to, not taken from.

During the first month Matt always seemed to be in skin-to-skin contact with one of his parents, usually mom but quite often me. After Martha nursed him I would frequently say to her, "Now it's my turn." She would drape our limp and satisfied baby over my bare chest and we would drift off to sleep together. I could sense that Matt knew that my body was different. His ear was over my heart, his chest and tummy were draped over mine, and his body moved rhythmically up and down with my breathing while my hands embraced his soft little person. My breath warmed his scalp as he nestled under my chin as if trying to find a warm corner in this new "womb."

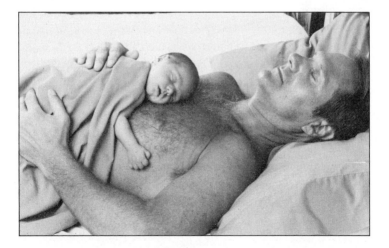

Dads can provide a warm fuzzy place to nap.

Father-Baby Addiction

We spent a lot of time together, buddies from birth. I began to feel what Martha meant when she said she felt addicted to our babies. I felt right when Matthew and I were together and not right when we were apart. But I realized that the ideal of full-time fatherhood was seldom achievable. I was plagued by that four-letter word, work.

Initially I was a bit envious that I couldn't sit at home all day and enjoy the luxury of just holding and nurturing Matthew. But I realized that I wasn't really designed to do that. Still, more than biology was at fault here. Our society totally ignores fathers—there ought to be a law granting new fathers paternity leave. Contrary to my previous history, I did shorten my office hours during that first month and tried to be at home as much as possible. And when I was home I was totally there—physically and mentally.

Father-baby bonding. I had an overwhelming desire to become addicted to our baby the way Martha was. After a few months, I was addicted to Matt, but it was still a different level of addiction than Martha's. Matt and I had a different relationship than did Martha and Matt. Not better, not worse, just different. She was close to him; I was close to him. But we were close to him in different ways.

I guess it was partly that we gave differently to Matt so he gave differently to us. Because we invested ourselves differently, he gave us different returns. Martha really gave Matthew part of herself. My giving seemed more indirect at times. I gave to Matt by giving to Martha and by giving to the rest of the family what they were used to getting from Martha. In this way she had more to give to Matt.

Martha has learned to achieve a healthy balance between attaching and releasing Matthew. Mothers who are very attached to their babies often have trouble releasing their babies to the care of substitutes, even to fathers. They have to prove themselves worthy of trust. Martha had no trouble releasing Matthew into my care because from the moment of birth, even before, I had proven my capabilities. I refused diplomatically to be labeled as a substitute mother. I was not just pinch-hitting for Martha, I had my own unique contribution to make to Matthew's development.

Mornings are my special time with Matthew. No matter how early fathers get up, babies seem to get up earlier. After nursing in bed, Matt is awake and aware and ready to begin the day—with me. Each morning we take a walk together to the bluff overlooking the ocean. Matthew soon grew to anticipate this early morning ritual. After awakening and nursing each morning, he would roll over and look up at me as though to say, "Let's get going, Pop." As we'd walk, Matthew would nestle his head under my chin, mold his body

Each morning Matthew and I walk together to the beach.

to mine, and relax into the rhythm of my walk. Early morning is such a prime time for babies. Matthew's little mind seemed so alert, although at times mine was still half asleep. These father-baby walks are special. Matthew may not remember them as he grows older, but I will never forget.

Withdrawal Symptoms

My addiction to Matt has grown stronger. I ache when I have to leave him. I get high when I'm with him. I suffer withdrawal when I'm away for more than a day. When I have to be away for one or two days to lecture or attend meetings. I go through an unconscious desensitizing process. I rationalize why I have to be away from Matt and justify my departure to myself so that I can depart with a minimum of guilt. It is almost as if I can't allow myself the luxury of developing a twenty-four-hour-a-day, seven-day-a-week commitment to Matt when I know that realistically I can't carry this out. Martha, however, can make this total commitment and she knows she can carry it out.

Fathers who are away from their kids are easy prey for all kinds of commercial enterprises. For me the worst is the airport gift shops. I frequently change planes in the Dallas airport where the omnipresent gift shops feature Dallas Cowboy uniforms for babies of all ages. If necessary I would pawn my watch, my ring, and even more intimate apparel to purchase Matthew another Dallas Cowboy sweatshirt. I measure my degree of attachment to Matthew by how closely I've guessed on the size of the sweatshirt.

As a Father Grows

During my preparation for attachment fathering, I had vowed to strike a balance between being, first of all, a committed father and, secondly, still being able to give enough time to my pediatric practice, university teaching, and lectures to parent groups. When outside commitments have piled up, I feel stretched, but my commitment to achieving a proper balance acts like a strong rubberband, pulling me back to Matthew and the rest of my family. The rubberband does not break. I don't let it get stretched that far.

Matthew is one year old at this writing. We have grown very close and he has taught me how richly rewarding the attachment style of fathering can be. My only regret is that it took me six children to discover this. While writing this book I realized that a father grows and develops along with his children. In other words, "Please be patient with me, my children haven't finished with me yet."

CHAPTER 2

Fathering before Birth

Fathering begins before birth. Like any good investment the earlier you get involved, the greater the return.

Some fathers may feel that they make their contribution to the pregnancy at conception; they think since it's mother's job to carry the baby in her womb, there's nothing more for fathers to do until the baby is born. Wrong! Mother carries the baby, but father cares for the mother. Also, recent discoveries about the capabilities of the unborn baby have revealed that fathers can and do contribute to the health and well-being of their unborn babies.

Caring for Your Baby before Birth

New and exciting research into the life of the fetus has shown that even before birth, a baby is a very competent little person. The unborn baby can hear, feel, see, suck, and do many of the other things that a newborn baby can do. A father can communicate with and influence his unborn baby in two ways: by talking directly to the baby and by caring for the mother so that she can better care for the baby.

Father Talks, Baby Listens

Recent research has shown that the baby in the womb can hear well by the sixth month of the pregnancy, if not earlier. Some researchers suspect that babies hear fathers' voices better than mothers' because the amniotic fluid transmits the resonant low-pitched male voice more easily than a higher, feminine voice (Ludington 1985). Fathers can communicate with their babies before birth. If you get your baby accustomed to your voice prenatally, you will have a head start on those many father-child talks you will enjoy in the years to come. Studies have shown that babies whose fathers talked to them before birth were more interested in their fathers' voices soon after birth (Ludington 1985; Verny 1981).

Laying on of hands. A custom my wife and I have enjoyed during pregnancy is the nightly ritual of laying on of hands. Every night before going to bed lay your hands on your wife's "bulge." (If you like, your doctor or midwife can show you how to locate the baby's head beginning in the sixth month of pregnancy.) Talk to your baby. Introduce yourself. Say, "Hi, baby. This is your daddy. I love you and I'm looking forward to seeing you." Let your loving thoughts flow with all the enthusiasm you would feel if you were pregnant, too. (One of the meanings of the word pregnant is full; a father can indeed feel full of love for his growing child.) At first you may feel somewhat foolish—a grown man talking to a lump!—but after your initial awkwardness, you'll begin to enjoy this nightly ritual. No one's going to hear you, except the people who count, and they'll understand.

The combination of a warm hand on mommy and warm words for baby affirms your commitment to these two special persons who depend on you after the birth. You affirm your commitment to your baby as a father and to your wife as protector and provider. This nightly ritual does wonders for your marriage relationship. A mother told me, "Every night I look forward to the special dialogue between my husband and the baby. Every time my husband embraces our baby I feel he embraces me too. I truly feel his commitment to both of us." In my conversations with expectant mothers, I have found that the greatest positive influence on the emotional well-being of the pregnant mother is the feeling that dad is truly committed to fatherhood.

What's in it for dad? Fathers who have practiced this prenatal bonding confide that they feel closer to their babies both before and after birth. One father put it this way:

> I'm hooked. I was so used to putting my hands on our baby and talking to our baby before birth that now that he's born, I can't get to sleep at night until I first lay my hand on the warm little head of our newborn and reaffirm my commitment to him as a father.

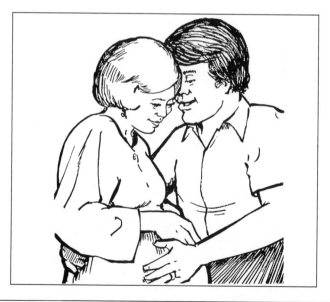

The "laying on of hands" before baby is born affirms
your commitment to your wife and child

The Care and Feeding of the Pregnant Mother

Besides talking directly to your baby, you can make a valuable contribution to the well-being of your baby by caring for his mother. The emotional state of the pregnant mother can affect the emotional state of the baby. When mother feels good, baby feels good. Mother and baby are a hormonal communication network; when mother is upset her body releases stress hormones which may cross the placenta and upset the baby. Researchers in personality development feel that a baby who is continually stressed during pregnancy may be born with an overcharged nervous system and have a higher risk of being a fussy baby (Sears 1985). The father-mother-baby care system works when you create a peaceful environment for both mother and baby. Here are some practical suggestions.

Take inventory of your marriage relationship. One of the greatest gifts you can give your child is to bring your baby into a home built on a stable and fulfilled marriage. Just as you periodically examine your job performance, take a good look at your marriage relationship. How can communication be improved? What unresolved issues should be settled? Remember that a pregnant woman's labile emotions are particularly vulnerable to feelings that the marriage foundation is a bit shaky or that dad is not really committed to the marriage or to fatherhood (Verny 1981).

Babies are not the only thing that grows during pregnancy; relationships grow, too. Pregnancy cannot help but affect the marriage relationship. Use the time during pregnancy to strengthen your commitment to each other. Pregnancy should have a maturing effect on the marriage and especially on dad. As baby grows so should your marriage and so should your maturity. For the first time in a man's life not only is another person—his wife—as important as himself, but a second person—the baby—becomes as important or more important.

Each day give your wife obvious "I care" messages. Many men sincerely love their wives but do not communicate their love very effectively. A friend of mine who does marriage counselling suggests that you must discover the things that communicate love to your mate. The language of love is different for each person. Ask your wife to make a list of ten things that she feels would be an expression of love from you to her. At the same time, you make a list of ten things that you think would communicate love to her. When the two of you compare lists you'll be surprised to see how far off you may have been. For example the first items on your wife's list might be: bring me flowers, give me little hugs several times a day, open the car door for me. One or two of these items might be on your list but appear down at the bottom. Your number one item may be taking your wife out to a nice dinner, which she may rate as number ten. To you the nice dinner is really an expression of love, but to your wife it may also be a statement that you want a night out, away from the humdrum of your household. The important thing is that you express your love in a way that your wife will understand. Next, to be fair, draw up the two lists from your perspective—what communicates love to you. It can be nice to find out that when your wife folds your underwear and matches your socks she's saying "I love you."

Respect the nesting instinct. During the final months of pregnancy mothers experience a nesting phase, a desire for stability especially in the home. This is no time to undertake major changes, for example, a job change or a move to a larger house. If a major change in the family situation is necessary or inevitable, try to make this change early in pregnancy rather than soon before or soon after the baby is born. To upset the nest is to upset the mother.

Prepare yourselves. Most new mothers take prepared childbirth classes to learn about labor and delivery and to make childbirth less stressful for mother, baby, and dad. Some fathers may consider these classes to be for mothers only, but this is not the case. Prepared childbirth classes benefit fathers in a number of ways.

First of all, you learn about the physical and emotional changes that take place in your wife during pregnancy. You learn why they occur and how you can be sensitive to them. My wife, Martha, is a childbirth educator, and I occasionally help out in her classes. I have noticed that even the most reluctant fathers gradually become more and more sensitive as the classes go on and the pregnancy nears its completion. Expectant mothers often share with me that one of the most important qualities they hope their husbands will develop during pregnancy is that of **sensitivity**. ("If only he were more sensitive to my needs," mothers often complain.) Sensitivity implies not only a genuine feeling of empathy for your wife but also being able to translate these feelings into actions that tell her that you truly care.

Prepared childbirth classes help fathers play an active, informed role in many of the decisions the pregnant couple needs to make in preparation for the birth of their baby—choosing a doctor or other birth attendant, a hospital or other birthing place. If possible a father should also attend the initial interviews with the doctor or other birth attendant.

Childbirth classes put you in touch with other expectant couples who may be going through similar experiences as you and your wife are. You'll benefit from the ideas and input of the other expectant couples in the class. You can learn about and discuss a variety of parenting styles as you and your wife make decisions about what will be best suited for your own family.

You will also learn how to support your wife during labor. When I attended childbirth classes early in my fathering career, fathers were encouraged to be "labor coaches." Dad was taught how to assist and encourage his wife and ease her discomfort during labor. While strong support from fathers during labor is indeed advisable, I now feel that men are often called upon to do a job all by themselves that they may not be equipped for. A labor support person, someone who herself has experienced birth and has some training in midwifery or childbirth education, can be an effective helper for both parents. Father can then assume the primary role of a loving, caring, and sensitive mate. (See the next chapter for a further discussion of father's role during labor.)

Father Feelings during Pregnancy

One of the highlights of pregnancy for fathers is feeling the baby move. Mothers experience fetal movement as early as the sixteenth week. Fathers can begin to feel movement around twenty weeks. Feeling this life together, your wife's hand upon yours and both hands upon your baby, may trigger the first solid realization that you are going to become someone's father. One of the earliest emotions you will experience as a father is a pride in your masculinity and your fertility. This pride is balanced by the reality that this new life will be completely dependent on you.

The meaning of the term dependent really sinks in as you realize that you have the responsibility of another mouth to feed. Just at the time the realization of your baby's dependence hits you, your wife may also show increasing dependence upon you. These growing responsibilities may make you question your ability to both take care of the baby and provide for the mother. Many fathers begin to worry about and exaggerate their inadequacy as a provider, worrying even before the baby is born about how they are going to be able to afford to send him or her to college.

Fathers have a wide variety of reactions to pregnancy. Some men actually experience pregnancy-like symptoms. I remember experiencing a sort of fullness during my wife's pregnancies. I felt more complete, as if life had taken on increased meaning. An entrepreneur friend of mine said that during his wife's pregnancy he "felt more rich." Some fathers, instead of enjoying the family pregnancy, regard this period as a necessary nuisance associated with having a baby. They tend to focus on the baby's arrival and subconsciously ignore the pregnancy and therefore, the mother. An expectant mother whose husband was coping with the many changes of pregnancy by simply tuning out the present and living in the future confided to me that sometimes she felt "more like a womb than a person."

Understanding Changes in Your Wife

It is difficult for many fathers, including myself, to fully accept the emotional changes that go on in a woman throughout pregnancy and the first year after birth. The physical changes in your wife are obvious, but tremendous emotional changes accompany these physical changes. The same hormones that are responsible for the development of the organs that nourish your baby now and after the birth (the uterus and the breasts) also affect the emotional state of a pregnant mother. They may cause a mother to feel and act more maternal and radiate a certain "glow." But these same hormones may often leave father feeling that his needs are going unnoticed.

For many mothers pregnancy is a time of identity crisis. They wonder about the future: "I am going to be somebody's mother, but what will happen to the me I know now?" You may find that your wife has ambivalent feelings about her pregnancy. She may feel proud that she has proven her fertility or she may be delighted that she is nourishing another life within her own body. But she may periodically have negative feelings: fear of becoming less attractive to you, fear of miscarriage, reluctance to leave her present job to care for an infant, anxiety about whether or not she will be a good mother. During the second trimester you may feel your wife becoming increasingly dependent upon you as protector and provider. She may crave periodic reassurance that she is still loved, that she still has value as a person, and that you're still committed to her.

Sexuality during Pregnancy

One of the most difficult tasks for expectant fathers is adjusting to the changes in their wives' sexual responsiveness. An understanding of the many physical and emotional changes that occur during pregnancy may help fathers be

more sensitive to the varying sexual responses of the pregnant woman. A woman's sexual desires vary throughout pregnancy because of fluctuations in hormone levels and the
physical changes in her body. Early in pregnancy, fatigue,
nausea, and gastrointestinal upset often make a woman less
interested in sex. Midway through pregnancy, a woman's sexual desires often increase; this, I feel, often parallels an overall
increase in her self-esteem. She feels more like a woman and
therefore can be a more exciting sexual partner. In the final
months of pregnancy most women's sexual desires diminish because of feeling awkward as a sexual partner and because they are afraid of inducing premature labor. Certain
medical conditions such as a history of premature labor, vaginal bleeding, or leaking amniotic fluid may preclude sexual
intercourse, although sex does not present a hazard to a normal healthy pregnancy. Your doctor can advise you further.

Your wife may feel that she has good reasons for her
diminished sexual desires because her body and her hormone levels are changing. She may, however, forget that your
hormones have not changed at all during pregnancy. As you
become more aware of your unsatisfied sexual needs, your
wife becomes painfully aware of her inability to satisfy them.
Mutual sensitivity to each other's needs and inventiveness
in sexual techniques are very useful at this time.

The final month of pregnancy will acquaint you with one
of the realities of new parents' sexuality—sex without intercourse some or most of the time. The final month of pregnancy and the first few months after birth bring to the surface
a basic difference between male and female sexuality. A
woman in the late stages of pregnancy or a brand new mother
may show a very strong sexual desire to simply be held and
loved, intercourse being way down on her list of activities
that bring sexual fulfillment. On the other hand, to the highly
sexual male fulfilled sex usually equals intercourse, and dad
may not be satisfied by simple holding and cuddling. These
differences in the final months of pregnancy help prepare
a father for the changes in sexuality that will probably occur after birth. Although there will be sex after birth, affec-

tion will not always lead to intercourse. (See Chapter 7 for further discussion of postpartum sexuality.)

Fears and Facts about the Future

The fear that there will not be enough sex after birth may give rise to fears about what other aspects of your marriage relationship are going to change. This may cause an otherwise jubilant father to focus more on what he is going to lose and how much he's going to have to sacrifice after the baby is born rather than on what he's going to gain and what he's going to have to give. Focusing on losses often dilutes the many present and anticipated joys of the expectant father. In reality, the birth of the baby should bring out the best in a man.

Nothing matures a man more than becoming a father. This may be the first time in a man's life that he has had to and has wanted to focus more on people other than himself—his wife and baby. It is normal to have fears and doubts about your get-away weekends and romantic candlelight dinners for two being temporarily changed to include "number three." These facts of pregnant life are why I sometimes use the term pregnant father. Pregnancy does more than grow a baby. It changes a father into a more sensitive, giving, and mature person. Pregnancy prepares a father for the real world of parenting.

You have often heard it said that it takes two adults to make a baby. I would like to turn that equation around a bit. In reality, it takes a baby to make two mature adults.

References

Ludington, S. M. Infant Stimulation Seminar, Anaheim CA, 1985.

Sears, W. The Fussy Baby. Franklin Park, IL: La Leche League International, 1985.

Verny, T. The Secret Life of the Unborn Child. New York: Dell, 1981.

CHAPTER 3

Fathering Your Newborn

I have always wondered why doctors take credit for the delivery of the baby. Does the doctor do the hard work of birthing your baby? It would be far more accurate to say that mother delivers the baby, father supports her, and the doctor assists and is on standby in case of medical complications.

Father does play a major role in the delivery of his baby. He "delivers" the mother from all those outside influences which interfere with the birthing process. He also is an active participant in the days following the birth as mother, baby, and father get to know one another and start their life together as a family.

Fathers and Birth

As the father of six children ranging in age from one to nineteen, I have experienced a wide range of involvement in birth. When our first two children were born, I waited pas-

25

sively in the fathers' waiting room while everyone else, it seemed to me, had an important part to play in the drama surrounding the debut of the person I had helped to conceive. As the size of our family grew, I was more and more determined to take part in the miracle of birth when each new baby arrived. In fact, when our sixth child arrived ahead of our birth attendant, I delivered—or I should say *my wife delivered* while I *caught* our new son.

Fathers have the right to participate in the birth of their babies. Exercise this right!

Be Sensitive during Labor

Fathers, your vital role in childbirth is to ensure, as much as you are able, that your wife has the opportunity to follow the natural signals of her body during childbirth. Attending prepared childbirth classes will help her tune in to her body's signals. Appreciate that every woman is equipped with the ability to sense and respond to what is going on in her body. However, the schedules and routines of most hospitals' labor and delivery units do not encourage mothers to truly follow their bodies' signals. This is where fathers can play an important role. For example, you should encourage your wife to move around during labor. Help her assume the laboring positions in which she feels most comfortable and that will help her work with her body effectively toward making progress in labor. Lying on her back during most of labor is not only the most uncomfortable position for mother, but it also may limit the amount of oxygen getting to the baby and slow the progress of labor. Embrace your wife during contractions, if she wants to be touched. Be tuned in to her needs. Be ready with pillows where she needs them for support. Rub her back. A small four-inch paint roller is excellent for back massage.

Spare Your Wife the Hassles

A laboring woman is not always rational and diplomatic with the attending medical personnel. She shouldn't have to be. A laboring mother should be tuned into her own needs and the baby's so that she can get on with the birthing. Any hassles with the attending personnel (paperwork, routines, hospital policies) should be taken care of by dad. When entering the hospital it helps for dad to let the medical personnel, that is, the nurse in charge, know that he plans to have a major role in this drama. Mother takes center stage at the birth, but dad is the stage manager and all the details should be cleared through him. Remember, a laboring mother is particularly vulnerable to suggestions that she may not be making progress as fast as the doctor or nurse wants her to ("Tsk,tsk! Still only two centimeters dilated!"). If you sense a negative and non-productive dialogue developing between mother and the attending personnel, step in and redirect the communication in a more productive and positive direction.

Dad's Involvement in Birth

When my wife went into labor I wanted to share her experience. I didn't want to feel the pain, of course; I was too chicken for that. But I wanted to experience, as much as I could as a male, the joy of giving birth. We had attended childbirth classes and learned a lot of technical maneuvers, but when the time came for me to "perform" I forgot most of what I had learned and decided to act on my feelings and simply love her through this labor. Whenever my wife showed that a contraction was coming on, I would embrace her as gently as I could. She held her arms around my neck while I held one arm around her and placed my other hand on "the bulge"—as I had affectionately termed this little person inside. As she labored I felt her arms squeeze me tightly and sometimes her fingers dug into my back. The more she dug in the harder I could feel her uterine muscles contract. Her panting and breathing patterns, her clinging embrace, and the ever-changing position of her uterus let my body sense, though indirectly, what her body was going through. She felt better having me there and I certainly wanted to be there. I really felt that I was playing a part in helping her labor progress. I got to "feel" her labor, too, and it didn't hurt me a bit. What a trip!

Is Too Much Expected of Dad?

Expecting fathers to take on the role of "labor coach" or "support person" may be asking more than they are equipped to handle. (After all, "real" men coach Little League baseball teams, not laboring women.) It is difficult for a man to help a woman tune into her body during childbirth. He is not biologically equipped to understand the process of birth the way another woman who has herself experienced childbirth can. I have come to believe that the ideal situation (and the ideal is not always achievable in our society) is for the father to assume the role he performs best—loving his wife, caressing her, saying caring things to her, taking care of the paperwork involved in a hospital birth—while a trained labor support person assists the mother in working with her body during labor.

A labor support person has some training and experience in midwifery or childbirth education. She is selected by the parents—not by the doctor or the hospital. Unlike a hospital nurse, she will stay with you during the entire labor, beginning at home before you enter the hospital, through shift changes in the labor and delivery unit, and during the birth itself. She can be an important source of support for both father and mother. Your childbirth instructor may be your labor support person. Above all, choose someone with whom your wife has a rapport. A trusted friend who has experienced birth might be a good choice.

REAL DADS COACH
LITTLE LEAGUE!

In my opinion the ideal birthing environment is one that allows the mother to respond to the signals of her body and encourages her progress in labor while providing the equipment, personnel, and technology necessary to handle unanticipated complications. In my opinion, the personnel needed for the birth should include: dad, to love and care for the laboring mother; a labor support person, preferably a midwife, to monitor the normal progress of the birth; and a physician on standby to handle any complications.

The Bonding Triangle: Father-Mother-Baby

When the concept of bonding at birth was popularized ten years ago, most of the attention was given to mother-infant bonding. Father was given a fine-print honorable mention. The early bonding studies have recently come under criticism for implying, perhaps unfairly, that the lack of a few critical minutes of contact with the baby right after birth may have lifelong effects on parent-child relationships. Despite the fact that the long-term importance of early contact is still open to question, it is generally agreed that early and frequent contact gives the father-mother-baby relationship a head start. Developing a relationship with your baby is based on a series of interactions, and the sooner these interactions occur, the sooner the relationship can begin to thrive.

The beneficial effects of early contact on mother and baby are well known (Klaus and Kennell 1976). The beneficial effects on the father-baby relationship are also beginning to be studied and appreciated. The term **engrossment** is used to describe the absorption, preoccupation, and interest that the newborn evokes from a father (Greenberg and Morris 1974). Engrossment doesn't describe so much what the father does for the baby as what the baby does for the father. A father who is ''engrossed'' in his baby is totally absorbed in the baby's unique features. He feels that his baby is distinctly different from other babies, and he can't wait to hold him, talk to him, and interact with him.

Engrossment ties into a favorite theory of mine: a baby can bring out the best (and the worst) in parents. Engrossment means more than involvement. One of the meanings of its root word, engross, is to "make large." Dr. Martin Greenberg, in his book *The Birth of a Father*, relates that not only does a new baby become a large part of a father's life, but fathers themselves feel that they have suddenly grown; they feel bigger, stronger, older, and more powerful. The father feels an increase in his sense of self-esteem and a stronger identity as a parent. I have noticed that a father in the delivery room often tunes out all the hustle and bustle of the medical personnel and stands spellbound, completely captivated by the little wet, slippery baby that he and his wife hold in their arms. While the mother is focusing totally on her baby, fathers view the mother-infant pair through a sort of wide-angle lens, perceiving the oneness that still exists between mother and baby, even though birth has changed the manner in which this oneness is expressed.

The traditional stereotype of fathers, especially new ones, is that they are well-meaning but fumbling and inept; they are afraid to touch their babies and exhibit very few intuitive nurturing responses. I do not think this stereotype is at all accurate. In fact, studies have shown that fathers who are given the opportunity and are encouraged to take an active part in holding and comforting their newborns are just as nurturing as the mothers (Lamb 1981). Fathers touch, look at, talk to, and kiss their newborns just as often as mothers. This indicates that if fathers are given the opportunity to interact with their newborns, they can be very nurturing. While nurturing responses may be less automatic and a little slower to unfold in fathers than mothers, fathers are capable of a strong attachment to their infants during the newborn period.

A period of private time as soon as possible after the birth helps get the family bonding process off to the right start. After the medical personnel have done their jobs and mother and baby are well, request some time alone with your wife and baby to revel in the joy of finally seeing and holding the product of your love. Embrace the two most important persons in your life, one arm around your wife and one around the baby snuggling and suckling at your wife's breasts. This is a special time of family intimacy which should not be interrupted by trivial hospital routines nor hampered by sedatives or other medications. A wise father will clear this request with the head nurse or birth attendant beforehand and will also ask that routines such as eye ointment or vitamin K injection for the baby be delayed until you have had this special time of family bonding. No one should interfere with the development of this triangle of love.

Many mothers feel very exhilarated during the first hour after birth and most babies are alert, which makes this a highly receptive time for parent-newborn communication. An hour or two after birth, all of you, mother and baby and father, will want to relax and even doze a bit as you recover from the most rewarding work you will ever perform.

Father's Role in Cesarean Births

In some births, a cesarean section is medically necessary. Depending on the type of surgery and anesthesia, mother-infant contact may be delayed. In this case father has the

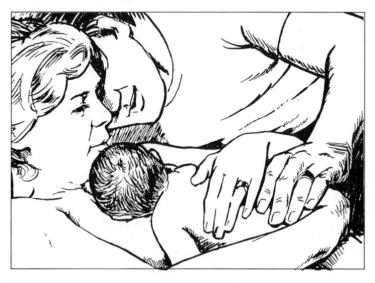

No one should interfere with this triangle of love.

first contact with the baby. It is vitally important that the baby immediately gets involved with the people who will be his or her parents, and with mother temporarily out of the picture, father must take over as second in command. In many hospitals fathers are allowed (and even encouraged) to be present at a cesarean birth. After the baby is delivered, a pediatrician usually performs any necessary medical care such as suctioning of mucus or administering oxygen and stimulating breathing. Immediately after the medical personnel have ensured that the baby has made a healthy transition into postnatal life and is breathing well on his own, father should be invited to hold and talk to the baby in the delivery room. (I advise you to clear all this with your doctor before the delivery.) Fathers who get their hands on their babies and take an active role in their care immediately after birth are the ones who find it easiest to get hooked on their babies.

Let me share with you a story about a father whose wife recently had a cesarean birth. Jim, a big strapping macho type of man, wasn't sure that he really wanted to get involved with a cesarean birth. After all, he thought, this whole scene was really a woman's thing and maybe he'd be better off in the waiting room till all the drama was over. Nevertheless, I encouraged Jim to accompany me into the delivery suite,

GET HOOKED ON
ME, DAD!

and after I had performed my pediatrician's duties and was sure that the baby was warm, pink, and breathing well, I encouraged Jim to accompany the baby and me to the newborn nursery. Jim was still in awe of all the technology surrounding the operation, but he obediently followed me. After I placed his baby in the infant warmer, I said to him, "Jim, I need to attend another delivery, and it's very important that someone stay with your baby and stimulate him, because babies breathe better when someone is stroking them and talking to them." I encouraged Jim to get his hands on the baby and talk and sing to him and rub his back. I promised to be back in about fifteen minutes. In spite of all the uncertainty characteristic of fathers who have been wrongfully portrayed as well-meaning but bumbling when it comes to handling babies, Jim bonded with his baby while I was gone. When I returned, I congratulated Jim and assured him that this initial investment was going to pay long-term dividends. The next day when I made my hospital rounds and went in to talk with Jim's wife, she exclaimed, "What on earth happened to my husband? I can't get our baby away from him. He's really hooked. I never thought I'd see that big guy be so sensitive."

Studies have shown that at six months postpartum, fathers of infants delivered by cesarean were engaged in more caregiving activities, especially in soothing the babies, than fathers of vaginally delivered infants (Lamb 1981; Rodholm 1981). Perhaps this is because of the extended early contact with their babies that many of these fathers experience.

Father's Role in Mother-Baby Attachment

Fathers are often confused about their role in the care of the baby during the first months. A newborn baby's main needs are for food and comfort, and most fathers feel unequipped and unable to satisfy these two vital needs. John, a new father, resolved his confusion about what he could do for his new baby this way: "I can't nurse our baby and

I don't always have the means to comfort her, but at least I can create a supportive environment which encourages my wife to nurse and comfort our baby better."

Though there may be an ideal way to create this environment and help baby and mother get organized, the ideal is not always achievable. (It certainly has not been in our family.) Nevertheless, it helps to know what the goal is and to aim for it as best we can. As a father of six, I feel that fathers, in some ways, have an even tougher job during the newborn period than mothers. Fathers have two jobs to do: caring for their babies directly, and indirectly caring for their babies by taking care of the mother.

Understanding Mother-Infant Attachment

In order to truly appreciate the vital role that father plays in the care and feeding of both baby and mother during the first month, it is first necessary for fathers to understand the unique bond between mother and infant. This attachment begins before birth. During the nine months of pregnancy, baby and mother develop a sense of oneness which is natural for mothers to feel because, after all, both persons are contained inside one body. But because mothers cannot see their babies in the womb, many mothers feel as if the baby is a bit of a stranger. Birth brings a sense of completion as mother and baby meet one another face to face. Attachment continues, birth having changed only the manner in which this attachment is expressed. One mother explained, "It helps me to regard my baby's gestation as eighteen months—nine months inside and nine months outside." Fathers can and should undertake the care and feeding of the mother during both the inside and outside phases of the baby's development.

After birth a mother's feelings about her baby oscillate between oneness and separateness. In some ways she regards the baby as a separate person; in other ways she still feels the baby is part of herself. There is a natural and healthy psychological transition from oneness to separateness that each mother-baby pair must make. If both mother and baby are allowed to experience oneness when they need to be one and separateness when they need to be separate, both members of this pair feel fulfilled. If mothers or babies are hurried into separation before they're ready or if their energies are diverted from each other, the normal design for healthy mother-infant attachment is threatened.

Bonding experiences at birth are not like some magical epoxy which cements the mother and child together forever; they simply give the relationship a head start. After fathering six children and counseling thousands of new parents I have concluded that parents need a minimum of two weeks of close contact with their new baby to start building their attachment to one another. Building a relationship with a person starts with a series of interactions with that person; you have to spend time with that person. When mother and baby share a "nest" and are in touch with each other they get to know each other better. They get used to each other. Fathers need to spend time with both mother and baby as these interactions take place and the family's bonding develops.

Fathers need to recognize that many new mothers are insecure about their mothering capability. Their intense love for their baby brings self-doubt: "I want to be a good mother, but will I be? I want to give my baby the best, but I don't know what the best is!" Both mother and baby are unorganized and uncertain as to what is expected of them. For the mother, two important persons help resolve the uncertainty and smooth out the problems in organization: the baby and the father.

Father Creates the Environment
Let's take a look at how mother and baby develop each other in a setting created by the father. Every baby comes endowed with attachment-promoting behaviors and features, for example, a round attractive face with penetrating eyes, a vocabulary of cries and coos, soft skin, cuddliness. These are features and behaviors which are designed to alert caregivers to babies' needs and to promote caregiver attachment. They are designed to cause the caregiver to want to

pick up and hold the baby. Every mother is designed with a sort of built-in receiver which picks up the signals of her own baby. The role of the father is to make it easier for the signaler and receiver to get together. When the baby nurses, the mother produces a hormone called prolactin. This is the mothering hormone. I also call it the "intuition hormone" or the "perseverance hormone." This interesting hormone may be what makes mothers intuitively more nurturing than fathers. If prolactin is injected into male experimental animals they act like mothers. Prolactin may make human mothers more intuitive, nurturing, and tranquil.

Picture the mutual giving that occurs between mother and infant as they get to know each other. The baby's nursing helps the mother produce the very hormone that helps her to be a better mother. The baby plays an important part in his own care by helping develop the intuition of the person who will care for him. When the baby spends more time in the mother's arms or at her breast, mother learns about the baby's personality by observing how he acts. She gets to know his smell, touch, breathing rhythm, sleep cycles, facial expressions, cries, and pre-cry signals. She witnesses every-

thing the baby does and draws conclusions about how the baby feels and what he needs from the way he acts and the way he signals. When the baby gives a cue and mother responds, they both feel better. This is how mother-baby harmony develops. The baby gives a cue; mother, because she is open to the baby's cues, responds. Baby likes the response, and because he has learned he will get a predictable response, he is motivated to give more cues. The mother-baby pair begins to enjoy each other. As one attached mother told me, "I'm absolutely addicted to her." Once this happens, the mother's responses become more spontaneous, her mothering skills improve, and the relationship flourishes.

Babies Need to Feel Right

What do mother and father do for baby? A newborn baby's sleeping, eating, and breathing patterns are disorganized. He feels uncertain and confused and this breeds a feeling that things are not right. As the parent-infant relationship unfolds the baby feels more organized. Being continually in a parent's arms, in touch with a parent, helps the baby gradually organize his behavior and become more certain of his environment. Baby knows to whom he or she belongs. When he learns that hunger is followed by feeding, distress by comfort, and cold by warmth, the baby learns to trust his environment. He feels right. A baby who feels right, acts right, and a baby who acts right is more of a joy to parent.

Take as an example the way parents respond to a baby's cries. Early in the newborn period, because the cry is so disturbing, the mother responds immediately to the baby's cries and picks him up and comforts him. Gradually she develops efficient comforting methods that work for her baby. As she begins to be better able to read her baby's behavior, she begins to pick up on the pre-cry signals—a certain way of squirming around or a particular facial expression. Mother responds to these signals the same way she would if the baby had begun to cry. The baby soon learns that he does not have to cry to get what he needs, and therefore he fusses less and becomes a "better" baby. Mother's responses taught

the baby to communicate better. The two are in harmony.
Mutual giving leads to mutual sensitivity. Being sensitive
is a crucial part of parenting; if I were asked to sum up the
causes of parent-child problems in one word, that word would
be insensitivity. When baby and mother are in harmony with
each other they become sensitive to each other. When one
member of this harmonious pair is upset, the other will also
be upset. When one feels right, the other is more likely to
feel right. (It naturally follows that a father should do what
he can to keep both feeling right.) As a pediatrician I value
this mutual sensitivity because I know that a mother who
is tuned-in to her baby's "feeling-right" signals will also be
more aware of the "feeling-wrong" signals and will not wait
until the baby is very sick before she calls me. Mother-infant
attachment is good preventive medicine. It is vitally important for fathers to understand and support this intense
mother-infant attachment and not feel threatened by it.

How Fathers Can Help Mothers and Babies Develop Harmony

Take time out.   A new father needs to take time out and
spend the early weeks focusing on his wife and baby. They

Sensitivity Grows

The closer my wife got to our baby the more sensitive
she became. I first noticed this sensitivity in the way she
responded to our baby's cries. His cries bothered her more
and more so that she could not stand to let him cry.
David's cries bothered me too but not as much as they
bothered my wife. After about a year of this sensitivity
I noticed that she was becoming more sensitive to me.
When I felt down, Susan would pick up on my feelings
quicker than she did before David was born. I think our
baby, in some way, taught my wife how to be more sensitive toward me.

---

need to spend as much time together as a family as possible. This is how dad gets to know his baby and how he learns to help his wife be a good mother. Spending time together helps dad become sensitive to his new family's needs. For some fathers, it's the ideal time to take their two-week vacation from work. Others may find they qualify for some type of parental leave as more and more companies are offering this kind of benefit.

At the very least, dad should cut back on any extra activities during the early weeks of his baby's life, skipping an evening sales meeting, declining an out-of-town trip, not volunteering for overtime hours, etc. It is worth the investment in terms of the future harmony of your family to make the commitment of spending time together in those early weeks.

Prepare the nest. When mother and baby come home from the hospital or birthing place (or in the case of home birth, immediately after birth), make the nest—your home—as conducive to mothering as possible. Take over the housekeeping, or hire some help if you can afford it. Because of the tremendous physiological and emotional changes going on in the postpartum mother, you will find her emotions very labile, to say the least. She is easily upset by the slightest untidiness in her nest. An otherwise minor upset, for example, a broken washing machine, may seem like an insurmountable obstacle which threatens to overturn the harmony of the entire household. My wife, Martha, is upset by even one dirty dish during the early postpartum period; usually a sink full of dirty dishes doesn't faze her. Keep the nest as tidy and as clean as possible. An organized environment helps foster an organized emotional state in mother and baby. It is a good idea to stroll around the house each day and take inventory of actual and potential problems that may upset the mother—and then take care of these problems. Remember that upsets felt by the mother may be transferred to the baby. An acronym for fathers to remember is TIDY: Take Inventory Daily Yourself.

Siblings. Toddlers and preschool children can be especially demanding during the postpartum period. They are accustomed to having mommy all to themselves and may feel threatened by the presence of the new baby, especially if your wife has been practicing attachment mothering. With other little ones in the family, it's even more essential for dad to take time off work during the baby's early days. You can help your child through this adjustment period. Entertain your toddler or preschooler with creative play: new games, trips to the playground, special toys. Help your child to feel that even though mom must spend a lot of her time with the new baby, dad is sure fun to be with.

Issue specific instructions for older siblings to pick up after themselves. Tell them why particular attention to tidiness is so important at this time. After all, they are future mothers and fathers. They should learn that the postpartum period is a time when the whole family *gives* to mom. It is a time for all those little (and big) takers to become givers.

Improve your "serve." Stan, a professional tennis player and new father, asked me how he could help with his newborn baby. I advised him to "improve your serve." Many of us fathers are used to being served by our wives. The postpartum period is a time when you can improve your service to your wife. Serve her breakfast in bed. Take a walk with the baby while mother takes a shower and has some time for herself in the morning, or during the notorious 4:00 to 6:00 PM fussy period. Give your wife frequent "I care" messages as you did during her pregnancy; try to make sure that your messages are such that she clearly perceives your meaning. Take over as much of the housework as you can or see that it gets done by someone else. Take the phone off the hook while mother and baby are sleeping and put a "do not disturb" sign on the door. Much of your service to your wife during the postpartum period involves guarding the gates against well-meaning but intrusive visitors who threaten to upset the harmony in the nest.

Fend off purveyors of bad baby advice.   Love for her baby makes a new mother particularly vulnerable to advice that implies that she might not be doing the best thing for her baby. She is vulnerable to any advice that is proclaimed as a way to make her baby behave "better" or any suggestions that her current style of mothering may do harm to the baby. Some mothers feel they can't win. Conflicting advice is confusing to even the most confident mother. It plants doubt in the mother's mind and makes her fearful that lasting harmful effects will ensue. If you sense that outside advice is upsetting your wife even slightly, put a stop to it, even if the baby-raising tips come from your own mother.

Be sensitive.   Be aware of your wife's needs. Many new mothers are reluctant to ask for what they need for fear of shattering their image as a perfect mother and appearing weak in the eyes of their husbands. Fathers sometimes have to figure out for themselves what mothers need. One mother told me, "I'd have to hit my husband over the head before he'd realize that I'm giving out."

"She's spoiling that baby . . . let him cry it out!"

Don't let outside advice interfere with your wife's
confidence in her mothering.

Be in charge. The overwhelming desire to be a good mother sometimes overrules a woman's ability to know her limitations. Many mothers try to keep up with their pre-motherhood activities. They fail to realize that they do not have enough energy to be all things to all people, maintaining the same social, financial, and other commitments they had before giving birth. My wife, Martha, teaches childbirth classes and in one of her classes she advises mothers to stay in their nightgowns for at least two weeks after birth, the nightgown being a signal to everyone that she is still recovering from giving birth. It's up to fathers to take charge of the house and be sure that their wives are not saddled with commitments that drain their energy. An exhausted, over-committed mother is likely to become a victim of postpartum depression or mother burnout.

Postpartum Depression

About fifty percent of all mothers experience some degree of after-baby blues. Symptoms include fatigue, outbursts of crying, anxiety and fear, insomnia, loss of appetite, lack of concern with grooming, a tendency to "make mountains out of mole hills," withdrawal from social contact, and often, a negative attitude towards the husband.

Fathers feel helpless in the face of their wives' postpartum depression. Because they do not understand the problem, they do not know how to cope with it nor do they know how to help alleviate it. Most postpartum depression is the result of too many changes happening too fast. It is natural that the excitement of birth is followed by a let-down. Consider all the changes that take place in a mother's body after birth. The mother's sleep cycles are disturbed. Her body is rapidly returning to a non-pregnant state; she is experiencing tremendous hormonal fluctuations as the levels of pregnancy hormones gradually diminish and the postpartum hormones take over. These physical changes bring changes in moods and feelings. I feel that the most important cause of postpartum depression is downright exhaustion. Everyone is making demands on the new mother.

Dad's Understanding Is Needed

When my baby was about six weeks old, I encountered my first bout of depression. After a long evening of trying to comfort my baby daughter, she finally fell asleep in my arms. I had been feeling sorry for her, but all I really felt was tired, trapped, and alone. I began to cry as I searched for the tender love that I was supposed to be feeling for my infant child. I knew that was supposed to make it all worthwhile. I put her in her bed, went to my husband, and cried on his shoulder for half an hour. He didn't know what to say as I babbled on about my feelings, so he just held me. That's all I really needed anyway, and then I went off to bed.

The next day, I packed up the three of us and we went for a picnic in the park. As Sarah slept nearby, Bill and I talked about our feelings. Since I had never really expressed my concerns, Bill had thought I was doing just fine, that I was strong and resilient from the beginning. What news!

He realized that I was very tired and was kept very busy caring for our little one. Since we both work from home, he sees what I do with her all day. He admitted that he could offer to take her and walk or rock her more often when that's all that the baby might need.

He had thought about my not feeling "in love" with Sarah and concluded that it takes more than just having a baby to love it as a person. Loving someone is much easier when you get to know them, and they give you something back, or at least have some personality trait that tugs at your heartstrings.

A newborn infant only knows what its physical body tells it, and then its only communication is one of five or six cries! The mother tries to interpret the cries, and gives, gives, and gives some more. There is comfort to a new mother in having satisfied some need of the child, but there is also a wearing down of the mother's patience and ability to deal with extended periods of mothering!

Bill and I reached an understanding that day that changed our lives. Since I came to terms with my feelings, I am more patient with meeting the needs of my baby, while getting to know her better each day and hence loving her more and more. And Bill has learned not to scold me for getting upset and irritated, but rather to support me with hugs and tender words for both baby and me during those trying moments. And since Sarah has started interacting with us more, with sure smiles and gurgles, there is no doubt that we love her very, very much. The housework can wait, and I no longer worry about being the perfect wife and mother. I just do what I can, and Bill helps out along the way.

Risk Factors for Postpartum Depression

Certain new mothers are more at risk than others of developing postpartum depression. Here are some key factors that place a woman at greater risk:

1. Coming from a high-profile career in which she has received regular feedback and a lot of professional recognition. This woman may have ambivalent feelings about changing her status from executive to mother.

2. A history of marital discord and the unrealistic expectation that having a child will solve marital problems.

3. A negative birth experience in which fear, pain, and lack of control predominated.

4. Mother and baby being separated a lot in the days after the birth.

5. A history of depression or of difficulty coping with multiple stresses.

6. Having a baby with a high level of needs.

Besides making an effort to understand postpartum depression, there are ways that fathers can prevent or ease the problem. I am reminded of the question on the television commercial, "How do you spell relief?" In the case of postpartum depression, I would spell relief F-A-T-H-E-R. Here are some practical ways that fathers can help avoid postpartum depression in a new mother.

Nesting. Keep mother and baby together as much as possible during the first weeks after birth and allow them to develop the mutual sensitivity and harmony described above. Respect your wife's strong nesting instinct. Mothers need a period of uninterrupted settling-in time with a new baby. Upsetting the nest during this time upsets the mother. This is not the time to move into a new house, begin a new job, or get involved in too many outside commitments or projects. If possible, major changes should be made either a few months before birth or a few months after, but not during this sensitive period.

Mother the mother. Your wife needs mothering, too. Try to take over or delegate to someone else the many energy-draining tasks which take away from mother's special time with baby. In many traditional cultures new mothers receive assistance from a doula, another woman who takes over the household chores and frees the new mother to be with her baby. A husband can be a doula to the new mother. So can friends. If someone asks if there is anything you need, don't turn down the offer. Suggest that the friend bring a meal over or help with household chores. You can also encourage your wife to get regular exercise and to eat nutritious meals and snacks.

Lend an ear. If your wife is having problems adjusting to the change from career to motherhood, help her feel that she has taken a step up on the ladder of personal worth and is doing the most important job in the world, mothering your child. Encourage your wife to voice her inner feelings. Does she feel inadequate and unprepared to be a mother? Is she angry that her birth and early mothering experiences didn't turn out as she had hoped? Sometimes a mother who, through no fault of her own, experiences a complicated labor and delivery may feel that she has "failed the course" because her birth experience did not go as planned. This sense of failure can often lead her to feel angry at herself and can carry over into feelings of inadequacy as a mother. Help your wife work through these feelings. Remind her that mothering takes place in the present and the future, which she can change, and not in the past which she cannot.

Encourage group therapy. Some zealous new mothers, wishing to devote themselves totally to their babies, withdraw completely from social contacts at the very time when they most need the support of others. The best of mothers, the ones who strive to be perfect, are the most likely to become burned out. They give and give and give and don't realize that they themselves are giving out. Point out to your wife that the traditional cultural model for a human mother and baby has never been a mother alone in a room with a baby. It has always been mothers and babies sharing their burdens and their joys. Encourage your wife to join a support group such as La Leche League early in the postpartum period or even prenatally. She may want to continue getting together with the group of mothers she grew comfortable with in your prepared childbirth classes. Make it easy for her to attend support group meetings even before she feels ready to venture out on her own: "Tonight's the La Leche League meeting. I've already ordered a pizza and after we eat I'll drive you to the meeting and pick you up afterwards."

Body image. Some new mothers expect that they will quickly regain their pre-pregnant figures and be able to wear all of their favorite clothes. These expectations are unrealistic, and consequently many women are depressed and frustrated by their postpartum bodies. There is so much emphasis on being slim and trim and fashionably dressed in our society that a new mother's self-esteem takes a real plunge when she is unhappy with the way she looks.

Encourage your wife to buy herself a new outfit, one that fits well and allows for easy, discreet nursing. This is a concrete way to let her know it's okay for her to look the way she does and you don't expect her to fit back into her pre-pregnancy clothes right away. Her mental image of herself will improve if she knows she can put on at least one outfit that fits and looks nice.

Your wife's body image is bound to be somewhat maternal for a while, and it will be important for you as her mate to accept and approve of who she is and how she looks. Nothing boosts a woman's mood more than to have the man she loves tell her how beautiful she is to him. I have actually heard some men tell their postpartum wives that they are too fat or too wide in the hips or otherwise unacceptable. They'll never know how damaging that can be to a woman's self-esteem. Of course, there will come a time when your wife's body begins to take on familiar lines once again. But it is not in your baby's best interest for your wife to lose large amounts of weight while she is breastfeeding. Keep this in mind if you are tempted to push her into losing weight. Of course, the time will come when she will welcome some constructive moral support for gradually getting back into shape.

Be a back-up caretaker. Some babies ask a lot of mothers. These high need babies take a lot of time and energy which naturally leads to some mothers giving more of themselves

DAD, PLEASE TAKE
GOOD CARE OF MOM.

than there is to give. Mother ends up exhausted and not much good to anybody. There should be a healthy balance in this taking and giving relationship, but sometimes the situation can get out of hand. Fathers are the ones who oversee this balance and can step in and fill baby's needs while mother takes some time to recharge. A new mother does not release her baby easily to substitute caregiving, even to her baby's father. A father has to prove his nurturing ability toward a new baby before a mother feels she can entrust her baby

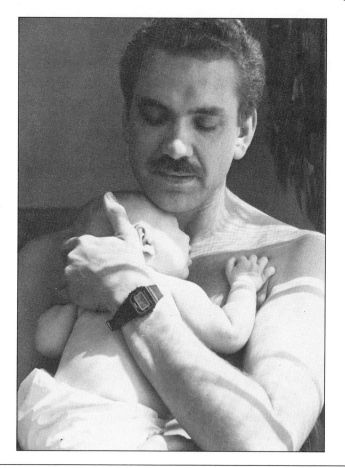

Dads can develop their natural nurturing abilities but it takes time and effort.

to his care. The more nurturing you are as a father, the easier it will be for your wife to accept your help when she really needs it.

Be sensitive to the symptoms and early warning signs of postpartum depression. Seek help before a simple case of after-baby blues progresses into a full-blown depression and you wind up being both mother and father to your baby while your wife recovers in the hospital.

The single most important way that fathers can prevent or alleviate postpartum depression in their wives may be summed up in one word: commitment—commitment to your wife as her husband and commitment to your wife's role as a mother.

Postpartum Depression in Father

Many fathers experience a bit of a postpartum let-down themselves. Fathers do not experience the hormonal and physical changes that mothers do. Their postpartum adjustment problems are mainly due to the increased responsibilities they face and the sudden changes in lifestyle that occur when a husband and wife become parents. There are financial,

1. Thou shalt not give up thy baby to strange care-givers.

2. Thou shalt not cook, clean house, do laundry, or entertain.

3. Thou shalt be given a helper.

4. Thou shalt remain clothed in thy nightgown and sitteth in thy rocking chair.

5. Thou shalt honor thy husband with his share of household chores.

6. Thou shalt take long walks in green pastures, eat good food, and drink much water.

7. Thou shalt not have before you strange and unhelpful visitors.

8. Thou shalt groom thy hair and adorn thy body with attractive clothes.

9. Thou shalt be allowed to sleep when baby sleeps.

10. I am your husband and will give you strength; thou shalt not have prophets of bad baby advice before you.

TEN COMMANDMENTS FOR THE POSTPARTUM MOTHER.

emotional, and sexual adjustments to be made. It helps to think of the postpartum period as another season of the marriage—a season in which more adjustments take place over a shorter period of time than at any other point in your life together.

Taking Care of the Baby

Most of this chapter has been about how a father can indirectly care for his newborn by taking care of the mother and how he can make it possible for the baby to bring out the best in the mother. However, father also has a very important and direct role in the care of the newborn, and the newborn baby can also bring out the best in a father. The father's engrossment with the baby after birth continues during the newborn period. His bonding with the baby should not be limited to those precious moments after birth. Although mothers do indeed have a hormonal head start on developing their intuition, I believe that fathers also have natural nurturing abilities and, if given the opportunity to develop these abilities, fathers can indeed participate in the care and comforting of their babies.

The more hours per day you as a father can spend holding your baby, grooming your baby, letting your baby fall asleep on your chest, talking to your baby, looking into his eyes, and attempting to soothe his cries, the more you will develop your natural nurturing abilities. I believe that we men have these abilities, but most of us have to work at developing our confidence in them.

References

Greenberg, M. and Morris, N. Engrossment: the newborn's impact upon the father. *Am J Orthopsychiatr* 44:1520-31, 1974.

Klaus, M. H. and Kennell, J. H. *Maternal-infant Bonding.* St. Louis: C. V. Mosby, 1976.

Lamb, M. E., ed. *The Role of the Father in Child Development.* New York: John Wiley, 1981.

Rodholm, M. Effects of father-infant postpartum contact on their interaction three months after birth. *Early Hum Dev* 5:79-85, 1981.

CHAPTER 4

The Breastfeeding Father

Pictures of breastfeeding usually portray only a mother and the suckling babe. Father, however, plays a major, though indirect, role in the breastfeeding relationship. In looking over my patients who are most successful at breastfeeding, one main factor stands out—sensitive and supportive fathers. My wife, Martha, decided to breastfeed our first child back in the 1960s when only about twenty-five percent of women chose to breastfeed. Even though I was a pediatric intern and had heard a little bit about the advantages of breast milk, I didn't offer an opinion for or against the idea and provided, at best, only passive encouragement. Now, after twenty years of marriage, six breastfed children, and fifteen years in pediatric practice I am absolutely convinced of the superiority of human milk for human babies. I want to convey to new fathers a feeling from the bottom of my heart:

*Do everything within your power to encourage and support
the healthy breastfeeding relationship between your wife and
your baby.* Breastfeeding is a lifestyle, not just a method of
feeding. Providing understanding and support for the breastfeeding pair is one of the most valuable investments you can
make in the future health and well-being of your family.

What Every Father Needs to Know about Breastfeeding

Species-Specific Milk

Just as the human mother is capable of nourishing her baby
for nine months in the womb, she is also capable of completely nourishing her infant for at least nine months after
birth. Each species of mammal makes a unique type of milk
that is especially suited to help the young of that species
survive and develop to their maximum potential. Milk, like
blood, has been perfected by nature in order that each species may function in its own particular environment. For example, seals and other cold-water mammals produce a milk
which is high in fat because seals need to maintain a high
level of body fat in their cold environment. The milk of cows
and other range animals is high in minerals and protein which
support the rapid bone and muscle growth necessary for
mobility and survival on the plains. Calves are up and running within hours after birth. Human milk contains special
proteins which promote the growth of the brain, the survival
organ of our species. Scientists are just beginning to discover
all the special substances in human milk that are uniquely
suited for the development of the young of our species.

Milk composition gives us a clue to the natural feeding
pattern of a species. In some species of animals the mother
is away from her young for extended periods of time, hunt-
ing prey or otherwise feeding herself. The milk of these species is high in fat, calories, and protein so that the young
can go many hours between feeds; the milk "stays with" the
animal longer because it takes longer to digest. This type
of species is known as an intermittent contact species. Human

milk, on the other hand, is relatively low in fat and protein, an indication that human babies naturally require frequent feedings throughout the day. For this reason humans (and other primates) are known as a continuous contact species. So when it seems as though your baby wants to nurse all the time, and it seems as though your wife wants to hold your baby all the time, realize that they are only responding to nature's design for survival of the species.

Advantages of Breastfeeding

Security.   Breastfeeding smooths the transition from prenatal to postnatal life. Fresh from the tension and trauma of birth, a baby put to his mother's breast feels no separation from his matrix, the place where he developed. He hears the familiar heartbeat, the familiar breathing, the familiar voice; he feels the enveloping warmth and touch of mother's body; his mouth finds a place to suck which helps the tension subside. Mother's face is right there, hovering eight to twelve inches from baby's face (the distance at which newborn babies see best) so that baby's eyes can drink in who she is even as he drinks in his first milk. Baby is secure, he is home, all is well.

Breast milk fights germs.   The very first milk your baby receives shortly after birth is called colostrum, which is very high in germ-fighting substances called immunoglobulins.

DAD, HELP MOM GIVE ME THE BEST MILK.

Your newborn baby is particularly vulnerable to germs, and breast milk is highest in germ-fighting substances at a time in your baby's life when he most needs this protection. Colostrum may be considered your baby's first immunization; it directly provides your baby with antibodies that fight germs. Mother's milk has sometimes been called "white blood," because it contains the same living cells that are found in blood. These white cells produce a special protein which coats your baby's intestines, preventing harmful germs from passing through into his blood.

Breast milk changes as your baby changes. Infant formulas are the same from day to day; they do not change. Your baby's needs are constantly changing, and breast milk changes to meet those needs. For example, fat accounts for the largest proportion of the calories in human milk, and it also is the most satisfying nutritional element. When your baby is hungry he suckles in such a way that he receives the hindmilk, a higher-calorie, richer milk. If baby is only thirsty or looking for a snack, he will suckle in such a way that he receives only the foremilk, a thinner, more watery milk. Breast milk is generally higher in fat in the morning when most babies are hungrier. The fat content of breast milk decreases as babies get older and require fewer calories per pound.

Easy to digest. Breast milk contains all the nutrients babies need in just the right proportions—fats, sugars, proteins, minerals, iron, vitamins, and enzymes. That's what makes it the perfect food for babies. There are enzymes in breast milk that help babies digest the fat almost completely. Because formula does not contain these enzymes, the fat in formula or cow's milk is not as efficiently digested. The excess fat passes into the stools and accounts for the unpleasant odor of bottle-fed babies' stools. The lower fat content plus differences in sugars and types of bacteria in the stools of breastfed babies accounts for their sweeter, milk-like smell. The more pleasant stools of the breastfed baby make diaper-changing more appealing to fathers. Formula-fed infants have harder stools that are more difficult to pass. Because breast milk has a natural laxative effect, the stools of breastfeeding infants are looser and cause less wear and tear on baby's bottom.

The protein in breast milk is also more easily and quickly digested than that in formula. Since the fat and protein in formula are not totally digested, formula-fed babies feel full longer than breastfed babies. This is why breastfed babies feed more frequently and why your wife seems to be "always nursing." Even the sugars are unique in breast milk. Human milk contains more lactose than formula or cow's milk and that is why it tastes much sweeter.

Breastfed babies are healthier. Breastfed babies have fewer respiratory and intestinal infections and fewer allergies than

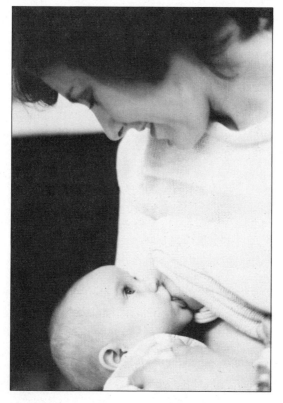

Breastfeeding enhances the responsiveness between mother and baby.

their formula-fed counterparts. This translates into fewer doctor bills for dad to pay. Breastfeeding may even lower your child's dental bills. The unique sucking action required during breastfeeding enhances the development of baby's oral muscles and facial bones. Orthodontists note that breastfeeding contributes to the improved alignment of your infant's jaw bone. Your baby's breastfeeding efforts will be reflected later in his face.

Breastfeeding ensures touch-time. As a pediatrician, I am convinced that every baby needs a certain amount of physical contact with his mother and father. Breastfeeding, by its very nature, guarantees that a baby will receive a half-hour of touching and snuggling at least every three hours during the day. The baby and mother must touch each other during feeding. The mother has to hold the baby close. She does not call in a substitute with a bottle, nor can she prop up a bottle and leave baby unattended. As a father, I am greatly disappointed that I cannot be with my babies all day every day. But it is comforting for me to leave for work in the morning knowing that my baby will enjoy a lot of touch-time during the day. While I am at work, I think often of the nursing pair at home, the most important persons in my life.

Breastfeeding improves the interaction between mother and baby. Recent research on infant development has shown that one of the biggest influences on babies' behavior and developmental skills is the mother's responsiveness. How the mother reacts is a very important determinant of how the child develops. When a baby gives a cue that signals hunger or distress and mother responds promptly to that cue by offering the breast, baby learns two things. He learns that he is competent—his simple signals produce a response from his caregiver. This gives the baby a sense of power. Baby also learns to trust that distress will be followed by comfort, that hunger will be followed by satisfaction.

Breastfeeding mothers respond to their babies more intuitively and with less restraint. The baby's signals of hunger or distress trigger a biological response within the mother (a milk let-down), and she feels the urge to pick up the baby and nurse him. This responsiveness rewards both mother and baby with good feelings. If a mother is bottle-feeding, her response to her baby's hunger or distress cues is quite different. She must initially divert her attention away from the baby to an object, the bottle, and take time to find and prepare it. Research has shown that a baby's memory span in the first six months is from four to ten seconds. The time it takes to produce a non-biological response, such as bottle-feeding, is usually longer than the baby's memory span. The bottle-feeding baby does not receive the same immediate reinforcement of his cues that a breastfeeding baby does. In my practice, I have noticed that breastfeeding mothers tend to show a high degree of sensitivity to their babies, and I believe this is a result of the biological changes that occur in a mother in response to the signals of her baby.

These hormonal changes account for the breastfeeding mothers who tell me that they feel "addicted" to their babies. How satisfying it is for fathers to create a supportive

Dad daydreams about the nursing pair at home.

framework which encourages this addiction to form. Fathers tell me that their wives seem generally more sensitive toward their babies *and* toward their husbands when they are breastfeeding. Mother's heightened sensitivity towards her baby carries over into how she relates to her husband.

Weaning—a Time of Fulfillment

Fathers are often exposed to peer pressure about weaning: "Is your wife *still* nursing that kid?" or "You'd better break that habit or the kid'll be coming home for a breastfeeding lunch when he goes to school."

Not only are more women choosing to breastfeed nowadays, but they are also choosing to breastfeed longer. Early weaning is an unfortunate practice in western society. We are accustomed to thinking of breastfeeding in terms of months and not years. I have a little sign in my office which says, "Early weaning not recommended for babies." One of the wisest investments you can make into the health and well-being of your child is to encourage breastfeeding for as long as both members of the nursing pair are willing and able.

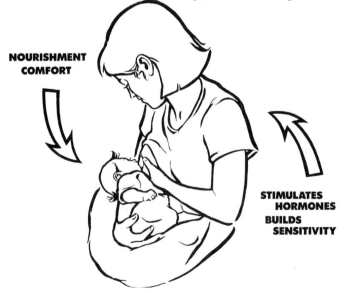

NOURISHMENT
COMFORT

STIMULATES
HORMONES
BUILDS
SENSITIVITY

Some of the most physically and emotionally healthy children in my practice are those who have been breastfed in terms of years. Children differ not only in how much breastfeeding they need, but also in how long they need it.

When our fourth child, Hayden, nursed until she was four years old, I began to study what is really meant by the term weaning. In the early days of history, especially in biblical times, weaning was a positive term. It meant "to ripen," as a fruit becomes ripe and ready to be picked from the vine. The term weaning was not associated with negative feelings of loss or detachment. Weaning was a festive occasion. When a child was weaned all the tribe got together and celebrated. They weren't celebrating the mother's independence ("Now I can finally get away from that kid"). They celebrated because weaning brought a sense of fulfillment. The child was filled with one relationship and was now ready to take on other relationships, as well as to begin formal education by the father and the elders of the tribe. In most cultures, weaning from the breast occurs when the child has acquired enough verbal skills to take on relationships with people other than mother, that is, at age two to three years. Weaning implies a smooth continuum from the security of mother to the security of other relationships, especially with father.

Life is a series of weanings for the child: weaning from the womb, from the breast, from the home to school, and from school to work. The pace at which children go from one stage to the next should be respected at all of these milestones. To hurry a child through one stage of need into another does not respect the child's dignity or his status as a little person with big needs. A term I've heard used by La Leche League members for nursing toddlers, little nursing persons, certainly demonstrates this respect. A child who is weaned prematurely from any childhood need and hurried into another stage may become a victim of what I call "diseases of unreadiness"—aggression, tantrum-like behavior, and mood swings.

Breastfeeding supplies both nutritional and emotional nourishment. On the nutrition side, most species of animals nurse their young until they triple their birth weight which happens in humans around one year. Babies who are weaned from the breast prior to a year often experience more illnesses such as ear infections, diarrhea, and allergies shortly after weaning. Weaning can mean more medical bills for dad. What about emotional nourishment? Years ago I wondered what the ideal time of weaning was for most children. While needs vary from child to child, in my experience if the environment is supportive and does not interfere with breastfeeding, most children will wean themselves sometime between two and three years. Some of the most physically and emotionally healthy children in my practice are those who have not been weaned from any need or relationship before they were ready.

In many aspects of parenting if you just let your parenting style flourish naturally in the way it was designed to, you can have a lot more fun. I love to hear the conversations that go on between the nursing mom and the little nursing person. They have a unique humor which can be enjoyed only during a limited time in a child's life. One of the funniest nursing conversations occurred in my office when two-year-old Vicky decided to have a little pick-me-up nursing before I began examining her. She crawled up on her mother's lap, nursed a few moments, and then exclaimed with great satisfaction, "All done, mommy's moo. No sugar, no caffeine!" Fathers have expressed to me their fears that extended nursing will make their child too dependent. Dads, let me reas-

EARLY WEANING NOT RECOMMENDED FOR BABIES!

sure you that your concerns are normal and usual, but un-warranted. Some of the most secure and independent children that I have ever known are those who have not been weaned before they themselves were ready.

Father's Role in the Weaning Relationship

Fathers play a major role not only in a good beginning to breastfeeding but also in a happy ending. Weaning means to cause a child to give up mother's milk and substitute other nourishment. Father is the source of the other emotional nourishment. There is a wide range of reasons why babies and mothers wean when they do. Father's role depends on the circumstances:

1. Neither mother nor baby is ready.

2. Mother is ready, baby is not.

3. Baby is ready, mother is not.

4. Both are ready.

When neither mother nor baby is ready.   When mother and baby are not ready to wean, but others are questioning the wisdom of continued nursing, father's role is to be a source of consistent and sensitive support. He should respect the signs that the breastfeeding relationship needs to continue. Ward off the naysayers who dispense bad advice and who lay guilt trips on your wife with remarks such as, "What, you're *still* nursing?" Take a protective and encouraging stand on what your wife is doing, even if the contrary advice comes from your own mother. Ignore your well-meaning but misinformed peers who imply that you should be "doing something" to rescue your wife from what seems to be an everlasting dependent relationship with your child. Avoid giving your wife mixed messages such as, "Oh, yes, you're doing the right thing in continuing to nurse our baby, but if you'd wean, we could get away alone." One of the most common dilemmas that mothers share with me is the confusion they feel when their husbands' wants conflict with their babies' needs.

When mother wants to wean (and baby doesn't). Some breastfeeding mothers reach a point when they have had enough, and either consciously or subconsciously they want to wean. However, after one or two years of nursing they may be so addicted to their babies or so committed to living up to their image of the perfect mother that they feel guilty about possibly causing emotional harm to their babies by initiating weaning themselves. Some mothers begin to feel that their breasts are no longer their own. One mother recently told me, "My two-year-old feels that these belong to her and not to me." (I've heard mothers express the same complaint about husbands' claims on their bodies.) Some mothers who have ambivalent feelings about weaning but deep down sincerely want to wean may be seeking affirmation from a trusted friend. Ideally, father should be this trusted person.

A wise baby who enjoys a happy nursing relationship is not likely to give it up willingly unless some other form of emotional nourishment is provided which is equally attractive or at least interestingly different. If your child is verbal enough to understand negotiations, encourage your wife and child to cut back on nursings, perhaps limiting them to when the child awakes in the morning and falls asleep at night. Managing this will require some creative input from both parents as you discover that keeping your child busy will probably also keep him from thinking about nursing. This is where father comes in. In order for weaning to proceed smoothly, baby must gain a bit of dad as he loses a bit of mom. And when the child needs comforting, the limits on nursing may have to come down temporarily.

It is much easier to effectively increase your involvement during weaning if you have been consistently involved in your baby's care since birth. Remember the pattern your baby is used to: distress followed by comfort, needs promptly filled. Up till now the breast has been baby's prime source of comfort. Father now has to come up with creative ideas for comforting that will substitute for breastfeeding, and this is not easy. The most difficult feeding for a child to give up is being nursed down to sleep. I remember one of my greatest challenges was to get our fifth child, Erin, off to sleep with my wife in the same room. I would use all sorts of dances and songs and cuddling tricks, but it was not until Erin was three years of age that I could finally sing to her and have her fall asleep without breastfeeding. I spent the rest of the night kidding my wife, "I finally beat the breast!"

When baby seems ready (but mother isn't). Realize that your wife may show a temporary grief reaction at the sense of loss of the nursing relationship. Be particularly sensitive to her labile emotions during weaning. This grief may be especially strong if this is your last child—her last nursing baby.

I do not pretend to fully understand the mother-infant bond, but I have learned to respect it. There is the occasional mother who truly has difficulty releasing her baby from the nursing relationship. Some mothers become possessive in wanting to hold onto this relationship. Some may use their children to fill their own needs (perhaps their need for intimacy, which may be lacking in their relationship with their husbands).

To some mothers, weaning means they will be turning over a larger share of their child's care into the hands of others, particularly the father. They may feel that the father has to prove his competence in baby-tending before they can release their child into his care. I have found in counseling mothers who have this problem that, while some mothers have not really given their husbands a fair chance to prove their competence, in other cases, fathers have been involved so little in baby care that the mother's hesitance has some justification. This unwillingness to release a baby into another's care is a byproduct of a strong mother-infant bond. Marriage counselors may not agree that this should be so, but I have found that the mother-infant bond is, in most families, stronger than the bond between husband and wife. The former is biological, the latter is by desire.

When a father proves his competence in child-tending and his willingness to be involved with his children, his wife feels that she can entrust them to his care. She will then be able to acknowledge the child's readiness for weaning. This book is written to help fathers develop that competence.

Baby Gets Confused

Our daughter is now three months old, and she has been exclusively breastfed since birth. I have been watching Marina thrive on her mother's care and milk and could see that they had a special connection during mealtime. Marina gives her mom an obvious look of love and absolute trust. I was eager to try feeding her bottled breast milk, thinking that I also would get that special look.

We had planned to start alternating between breast and bottle feedings, working up to a time when Marina could be left with a sitter.

Mom used a breast pump and stored a few ounces. The time seemed right; Marina was giving out her usual hunger signals and her mom was away, due back in about thirty minutes.

We sat down with the bottle and got comfortable. Marina took the nipple. Her eyes lit up. She began to gaze up at me the way I had seen her gaze at her mother. When she saw me, the joyful look vanished and was replaced by a look of total confusion that turned immediately into a look of pure terror. She refused to take the nipple and gagged when it touched her lips.

She began to cry and would not be comforted. She cried harder than she had ever before or since. She cried like that until her mom got home (early, thank you God) with the Real Thing.

I haven't tried that again. When she gets older, I'll try again and I know that it will work sooner or later. For now, we are very happy that Marina is being breastfed. After all, it is the natural way. Its obvious advantages (happy, healthy mother and baby) far outweigh any inconveniences there are; in fact, they all seem minor and easily lived with.

When both are ready. Normal baby-led weaning may occur somewhere between nine months and four years, depending on both the baby and the mother. Around one year, some babies become so busy with running around and exploring that they don't seem to need to suck. The older child is verbal enough to tell you when he or she is ready to wean. Our daughter, Hayden, at four years of age, said during Martha's pregnancy with Erin, "I don't like the taste of your milk anymore." Erin, at age four years, when given a choice between a bedtime story and a bedtime nursing said "I'd rather have a story. I don't want to nurse any more anyway." Martha was surprised that Erin chose the story.

Should Father Give Baby a Bottle?

With the trend towards increasing participation of fathers in the care of their babies, new parents frequently ask me if it is all right to give the breastfed baby an occasional bottle so that father has an opportunity to feed the baby. I discourage supplemental bottles especially during the first month because of the risk of disturbing the breastfeeding harmony that mother and baby are working so hard to establish. Instead I encourage fathers to understand, respect, and support the uniqueness of the breastfeeding relationship; this will help to keep them from feeling left out of baby care. There are plenty of other important ways for a father to participate in his baby's care, things like comforting and playing with the baby, giving baths, holding and rocking the baby. And certainly father can look forward to feeding solid foods to the baby when he is old enough. In the meantime, supplemental nourishment from dad should go to the mother.

In some breastfeeding families, fathers do give an occasional supplemental bottle (preferably of expressed breast milk) because the mother is working part-time or for some other reason has to be away from her baby. Here are some tips for those fathers or for fathers in bottle-feeding families who want to become involved with feeding. Watch your wife carefully as she feeds the baby and attempt to mimic what she does when you give a bottle. Hold your baby close to your torso, preferably within an eye-to-eye distance of twelve inches. Look into your baby's eyes as you give the bottle. Give your baby skin-to-skin contact during the bottle-feeding by holding baby's bare body (except for a diaper) in your bare arms. Baby should touch as much of you and you should touch as much of baby as possible during the feeding. Talk to, caress, and groom your baby. Concentrate on the baby as the baby is concentrating on both you and the bottle. Both members of the pair should feel that there is a person at each end of the bottle.

CHAPTER 5

Understanding and Enjoying Your Baby's Development

There are "Mommy and Me" classes everywhere, but try to find a "Daddy and Me" class. There aren't any. Fathers often miss many of the joys of growing with their babies, but fathering doesn't have to be that way. If you know a little bit about what to expect, you can better enjoy your baby and really get hooked on being with him. Knowing your baby's preferences at each stage of his development will help you interact with him. If you observe closely the fascinating changes your baby goes through during each stage, you'll appreciate his capabilities and his accomplishments all the more. Baby and father influence each other's development. By discovering fun things to do together, you'll enhance your baby's development and strengthen your own attachment to your child.

I must confess that I missed many of the joys of the first year with our first five babies. I am a slow learner. When our sixth child, Matthew, was born, I decided to immerse myself in enjoying his growth and development. I spent a couple of hours each day witnessing the magnificent physical and emotional changes in this unfolding little person. I kept a daily diary of all the new things he did, how one skill led to another. My involvement in Matthew as a baby had an enriching effect on my growth and development as a father. My only regret is that it took six children before I discovered how exciting babies can really be. Much of what I will share with you in this chapter is what I learned during my year with Matthew.

A day in the life of your baby. One way to enjoy and follow your baby's development is to take a day every two or three months and try to spend most of the time that day with your baby. Use a notebook or a pocket tape recorder to record what your baby does: every different kind of movement, facial expressions, likes and dislikes, sleeping and eating patterns. Not only will this exercise increase your enjoyment and awareness of the changes in your baby, but it will also increase your ability to observe and respond to your baby.

Birth to Three Months

Tim, a new father, confessed, "I just don't understand babies. I don't know what they're supposed to do when. They confuse me. I think I'll just wait until our baby gets a little older when he can talk and tell me what he feels." If he ignores his baby's first year, Tim will miss out on a lot. If, instead, he becomes involved with his baby right at the outset, he could lay the foundation for a deeper understanding of his child during later years. It is true that it is difficult for fathers (and often mothers) to figure out what a baby is thinking and feeling, but increasing your powers of observation can help you learn to decode your baby's actions.

What Your Baby Sees

A newborn's visual acuity is estimated to be around 20/300. This means that what an adult can see clearly from 300 feet away, a baby can only see clearly at 20 feet. Because of your newborn's limited visual ability, you may feel that you're not really connected to your baby when you try to maintain eye-to-eye contact. A newborn's vision develops slowly, as if the lens on a camera was being slowly brought into focus. In the first two weeks, your baby can see you, but your image is a bit fuzzy.

Around two weeks of age, you will notice that your baby begins to stare at you longer. If you are within twelve to eighteen inches of his face, you are in focus. If an object is closer than eight inches or farther away than twelve inches, the newborn's image of it will be somewhat blurred. To determine the distance at which baby can see your face most clearly, move him toward and away from you at a distance between one and two feet. The point at which your baby stares most intently at your face is the distance at which you are most in focus. You may also notice that your baby's eyes fix on your eyes for a fleeting second or two when he scans your face. Even though your baby seems to temporarily focus on your face, his eyes will continue to move independently most of the time; he seldom seems to be looking at you with both eyes. Because they cannot use both eyes together, newborns have poor depth perception.

In the early months babies become bored easily and quickly lose interest in static figures. It takes a constantly changing image to hold their interest. This is one reason that the human face holds such a unique attraction for babies. Researchers have shown that newborns pay closest attention to images that have the characteristics of a human face: contrasting light and dark areas, movement, roundness, and responsiveness to baby's own expressions. It has also been recently discovered that in the first few months infants are most attracted to images with vivid light and dark contrasts. Again, the human face fulfills the requirements. Fathers can easily capture the visual attention of their babies. There is usually plenty of light and dark contrast in father's face, especially if he has dark hair, a mustache, or a beard. During the first month babies see things primarily by scanning them; their eyes are always in motion. In the second month you will notice that your baby stops and stares at you for a few moments, and this may help you finally feel connected to your baby. In the second month babies can see more of their world and see it more clearly. Your baby will tend to stare at you longer, as if studying your face. It's a beautiful feeling when baby looks into your eyes and seems to say, "Hi, Dad." Now is the time when dads and babies can begin to play the imitation game. Open your mouth or eyes wide or stick out your tongue. These facial gestures are fascinating to a baby. They tend to hold his attention, and with a great deal of persistence and patience, you may get your baby to imitate them. Visual games help your baby get to know your face. They also help you develop the ability to hold the attention of your baby. Developing this holding power with the baby will enable him to enjoy longer play periods with you without losing interest.

A Fuzzy Face Can Be Great Fun

For those of you new fathers or fathers-to-be who have beards, and are thinking of shaving them off, you might want to think twice about it. Being a new father myself with a daughter two weeks old, I had no idea a baby could have so much fun with my fuzzy face. When I hold my baby close to me she stares at my hairy face, it's like a small entertainment center for her. It seems to toy with her senses—she looks at it, she touches it, she even smells it. She has a way of telling me how my beard smells with her expression. As far as touch goes when she feels my beard, she feels her own face, too. I guess she is wondering if she'll look the same. And, if some day your baby wakes up crying, just hold her next to that warm, fuzzy face and as she nuzzles into that comfortable, safe spot, chances are pretty good she'll stop crying. I think that's a pretty good reason for keeping my beard.

You can capitalize on the visual appeal of your face by placing an eight-by-ten black-and-white photo of yourself alongside of baby's usual sleeping place. The baby then awakens to the visual image of his or her father, even when you can't be there personally. Continued exposure to the image of your face during the early months reinforces your importance in baby's environment.

What Your Baby Hears

Newborns can hear very well, but they are more sensitive than adults to loud and startling sounds. Don't be disappointed if your baby seems to show a preference for mother's voice. Tiny babies do prefer higher-pitched female voices, particularly their own mother's. But take heart. Your voice does fascinate your baby. Men often talk in less sharply defined ups and downs and crescendos and decrescendos than do women. You may notice that sometimes your baby will be calmed by the low-pitched, crooning, somewhat monotonous tone of your voice.

Baby can awaken and see Dad's face.

Singing to your baby not only has a calming effect but also may stimulate his development. Researchers have suggested that singing stimulates more of a baby's brain than simple talking. When you sing to your baby, the lyrics are processed by the left half of the brain while the melody affects the right half. Each day during Matthew's first year he and I would have our special walking and singing time. I would nestle him in my arms with his head under my chin or, as he got older, place him on my shoulder, and we would take a ten- or fifteen-minute walk while I sang to him. You will notice that your baby prefers certain tunes. Remember which ones these are and repeat them as often as you can. You will notice that your baby shows subtle signs of anticipation when you begin a favorite tune. The eyes will sparkle and the whole body becomes alert. After a few months you will have developed an interesting repertoire of father-to-baby songs. Your baby will love the songs you make up as much or more than the songs you dig out of your memory. Matthew has really enjoyed the "Daddy Loves Matthew" song that I made up—and I'm no songwriter!

Besides singing, babies also enjoy music—the right kind of music. You can play records, tapes, or FM stations on the radio for your baby. Babies usually enjoy classical music with gentle mellow sounds; babies are often bothered by loud rock and roll. (Unfortunately, as the father of two teenage boys, I can testify that children's musical tastes change drastically between infancy and adolescence.)

How to Talk with Your Baby

During the first six months, your baby will find conversations with you to be very stimulating. Talking with your baby fulfills all of the four "R's" of infant stimulation: rhythm, reciprocity, repetition, and reinforcement. Recent research has shown that mothers, in general, seem to be able to communicate better with their babies and hold their attention longer when engaging in conversation. There is, indeed, an art to communicating with a baby during the first few months. While this often comes intuitively for mothers, it may be more of a learned behavior for fathers. Here are some tips to help fathers enjoy talking with their babies.

You may be amazed by how much a newborn can communicate when you learn to talk and listen in a way that he can understand. Video-analysis of mothers talking to their newborns shows the babies moving their heads in a rhythm synchronized with their mothers' speech. Mothers develop **reciprocity** in their conversations with their babies. This means that mother and baby take time to listen to each other as well as to initiate communication. Mother talks to baby in short bursts and pauses and then waits for baby's response. Analysis shows that the length of time mother pauses between bursts of language exactly equals the length of the response from her baby. Thus what seems like a monologue to a casual observer is really a dialogue. Although the baby doesn't talk, the mother behaves as if the baby had responded. Baby and mother learn to take turns: mother talks while baby listens, then mother listens while baby responds.

Within the first few months, mother and baby develop the ability to hold each other's attention. Holding a parent's attention and eliciting a vocal response make the baby feel competent. In the first few months, the parent initiates the sounds, and the baby responds with his own sounds and gestures. Later on, baby initiates and the parent responds. The parent's response motivates the baby to continue initiating. Having the ability to initiate a social exchange makes the baby feel competent and helps him develop a sense of self-esteem, an important factor in personality development.

Look, talk, then touch.   Fathers can learn to converse with their babies the way mothers do, but it takes practice and patience. Because fathers seldom have the luxury of long periods of unscheduled time with their babies, they are prone to over-stimulating their infants. They rush in and initiate playful interactions too quickly. This eagerness and impatience may agitate more than stimulate. Learn how to approach your baby—the look, talk, and touch sequence. First, establish eye contact and then begin talking before you pick your baby up for play or more conversation.

Watch for cues. Babies are not always in the mood for interaction. If you learn to identify what state of alertness your baby is in, you will know when he is most receptive to your conversation. There are three main states of alertness: sleepy or drowsy, when the baby is drifting off to sleep or just waking up; quiet alert, when the baby's eyes are open and he is attentive to what's going on around him; and active alert, when baby is awake but flailing his arms and legs around and not looking at any object or person with any consistency. Babies are most receptive to interaction with others in the state of quiet alert. Watch for your baby's cues: smiling, making eye contact, reaching out with his hands. These cues mean that your baby is ready to engage in some father-baby conversation.

Babies listen and respond better if you hold them upright, approximately twelve inches in front of your face. Leaning over the crib or bassinette and talking to a baby who is lying on his back is not an effective way to communicate, although it is a favorite shot for photographers and moviemakers.

Watch for stop signs. Babies also show signs of wanting to end the conversation: vacant staring, turning the eyes and head away from your face, a furrowed brow. These indicate that the baby has had enough for now. Fathers may take longer than mothers to recognize signs of disengagement, again because of their eagerness and impatience.

Avoid bombardment. Babies have short attention spans, perhaps only four to ten seconds. Short, frequent, playful interactions are more meaningful than forced, long interactions. Strike a balance between arousing the baby and helping him settle down. This helps him organize his behavior. Visual stimulation is especially tiring. Watch for cues that your baby's attentiveness is waning and he is losing interest. Learning when not to stimulate and talk with your baby is also an important part of communication. Understanding your baby's signals and moods early in infancy paves the way for more effective communication later on by teaching you to respect your baby's feelings.

Tub Tip

One way fathers can enjoy their babies (and be a help to their wives at the same time) is to take the baby into the bath tub for a nice warm, skin-to-skin soak together. Baby can lie on your chest, half in and half out the water. (Keep the water at an even temperature with a slow trickle of warm water from the faucet.) You can stroke the baby and slosh water gently over his limbs and torso. Besides getting clean, the baby will learn to enjoy water and will become mellow and ready to nurse off to sleep. This is often a sure way to soothe a fussy baby, and it will be very gratifying indeed for you, dad, to see your little one go from being upset and unhappy to lying stretched out and limp from this father-administered therapy.

Holding Patterns

Mothers and fathers carry their babies differently and babies enjoy the variety of creative holding patterns that fathers come up with. A recent study in Montreal showed that infants who were carried more cried fifty percent less (Hunziker and Barr 1986). The following are time-tested ways of carrying babies that I have enjoyed with our own children or learned from the fathers in my practice.

Cradle hold. The cradle hold is the carrying position that is often a favorite of mothers, especially if they are breastfeeding. Babies do not seem to enjoy this position as much with fathers since they usually associate it with nursing. They may squirm a lot and become frustrated when father doesn't come through with what they expect.

The front cuddle. Place baby in your arms or in a carrier and drape his arms and legs around your chest and your waist with his head resting over your heart and your hands supporting his bottom. The benefit of this chest-to-chest position is that there is a lot of body contact. That's what makes it so special.

The neck nestle. By placing baby in the front cuddle and lifting him up a bit until his head nestles into your neck and your neck and chin drape over baby's skull, you will have found one of the most comforting and calming of holding patterns. In the neck nestle, father has a slight edge over mother. Babies hear not only through their ears, but also through the vibration of their skull bones. By placing baby's skull against your voice box in the front of your neck and humming or singing to your baby, the slower, more easily felt vibrations of the lower-pitched male voice will often lull baby right to sleep. An added attraction of the neck nestle is that baby feels the warm air from your nose on his scalp. Experienced mothers have long known that sometimes just breathing onto their babies' faces or heads will calm them. They call this "magic breath." My children have enjoyed the neck nestle more than any of the other holding patterns.

The football hold. Tucking your baby under your arm like a football is particularly effective for soothing the colicky baby who has abdominal discomfort. Drape your baby stomach down over your forearm, head in the crook of your elbow and legs straddling your hand. Grasp the diaper area firmly while your forearm and hand press on baby's tense abdomen. This position is also called the **colic carry.**

Bending positions. Some babies, especially tense ones, settle best in the bent position. Flex your baby's legs against your chest, supporting his back with one hand and his neck with the other. Bending baby at the hips often untenses baby's whole body. Hold the back of baby's neck and not the back of his head. (Some babies will tense and arch more when pressure is applied to the backs of their heads.) You can tell when a baby is relaxed by watching the arms. When they begin to dangle straight down (the **limp limb** sign), baby has settled and is comfortable. In the first few months babies settle best by being bent toward you, face to face. From three to six months babies often settle best when they are bent away from you; they like to see what is going on around them.

The pushing-off position. Around the third month you may notice that your baby is not content to nestle very long. If his feet are perched on your hands he will naturally want to push up and peer over your shoulder. Babies like this position because they can exercise their legs against your hands while at the same time they can explore the world over your shoulder.

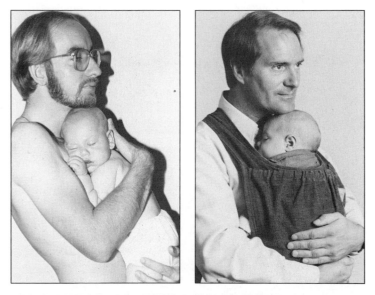

Two versions of the neck nestle.

The shoulder drape. If baby is particularly keen on what is going on behind you, drape him over your shoulder. Sometimes babies enjoy the pressure of your shoulder against their abdomens in a sort of burping position, especially if they have colic or gas.

The shoulder ride. When babies' back and head control is developed enough so that they can sit erect (usually around five to six months), they enjoy riding on dad's shoulders. This riding position gives them a more realistic perspective on the world around them; they begin to see things from your point of view. Older babies will often enjoy this riding position for a longer period of time than other positions because they are less restrained and have a 360 degree view of their world.

The sidesaddle position. At around five or six months, babies begin to prefer being carried on your hip to being in the front carrier. This position gives them more freedom with their hands and allows them to turn their heads and see in front and in back. This position is especially beneficial for

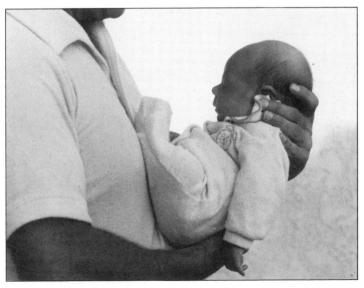

Bending baby can help him relax.

fathers with back trouble since most of baby's weight is squarely on your hips. Some baby carriers are designed to be used in the sidesaddle position.

Backpacking. When babies become too large or too squirmy for the sidesaddle position, they can graduate to a backpack, a baby carrier with a frame for extra support and better weight balance.

Baby Carriers
I am glad that there are a myriad of baby carriers on the market because most families need more than one. Some carriers work better for front-carrying positions, others for

Older babies love the shoulder ride.

side-carrying or back-carrying. Mom may prefer to use one kind of carrier; dad may prefer a different kind. If possible, try to have two baby carriers, one for mom and one for dad. This will keep you from constantly having to readjust the straps of the carrier to fit your body. This was a source of tension in our household; whenever my wife went to put on the baby carrier she found that the straps were too large for her—because I had just finished using it.

Dads, get used to wearing your baby in a carrier. While there are times when babies just need to be left on the floor to kick off steam, most of the time they love to be carried. After all, babies don't really learn much lying on their backs and seeing the world from the bottom up. Picture instead what babies experience when you wear them. When babies are carried, they see things and you see them. They get used to your body, your voice, your rhythm of walking, your odor, your touch. Most babies get to know their mothers' bodies, but few really get to know their fathers'. Early on, baby may not settle as well when carried by you as when your wife carries him. After all, he has grown attuned to the rhythm of your wife's walking during the nine months he spent *in utero*. You have a different style that baby will grow to appreciate. The more you get used to wearing your baby, the more you will begin to appreciate that your baby is actually a part of yourself. You feel right when you and your baby are together and don't feel right when you are separate. Mothers express this feeling as "I'm addicted to my baby." Most fathers miss out on this beautiful attachment. There is no reason why we dads should miss out on what babies have to give us.

Become a Diapering Father
I have always suspected that babies don't like wearing diapers any more than I like changing them. They certainly don't like to hold still during diaper changes. Here are some tips that will cut down on the hassles of changing babies' diapers.

Support for breastfeeding. Encourage your wife to breast-feed your baby for as long as possible. Breastfed babies' stools do not have an unpleasant odor and are less offensive to queasy fathers.

Setting the stage for the event.   Set up a pattern of pleasant behavior that baby can associate with diaper-changing. This will put him in a more receptive mood. Sing one of your baby's favorite songs right before changing his diaper or dangle a favorite toy from your mouth (your third hand).

Safety tips.   Beware of babies on changing tables. It takes a baby exactly one millisecond to roll off a counter or changing table while your back is turned or you are reaching for a diaper or a pin. And don't hold diaper pins in your mouth. Your baby will imitate this dangerous behavior.

Make it easy on yourself.   I have often felt that diaper pins are part of a subversive plot of mothers against their husbands. I don't like them and they don't like me. Use disposable diapers with plastic adhesive tape. If you prefer cotton diapers, use clips to fasten them or place them inside cloth diaper covers with Velcro closings.

There are many different kinds of baby carriers.

Make faces. Funny facial gestures and contortions will distract your baby. He will focus on your face rather than on what you're doing to clean up his bottom. Diaper changing is a social event, a time when fathers and babies share feelings. Baby senses that father, fumbling though he may be, cares about his bodily needs; fathers often sense that babies appreciate their efforts.

Be creative. With an older baby you may need to go to great lengths to distract attention away from the diaper-changing activity. What has worked best for me is changing my one-year-old son Matthew's diapers on a skateboard. The skateboard is one of his favorite toys, and he loves to push it along the floor. In his mind anything associated with the skateboard must be all right. The only way I can get him to hold still during a diaper change is to place him on a towel-covered skateboard.

Toys for Tiny Babies

Classes and toys do not a super-baby make. During the first few months, parents are the baby's primary playmates; however, appropriate toys are a welcome addition as baby's interests widen. When you select toys, look at them from your baby's point of view and take into account what he enjoys and is capable of doing at a given stage of development.

For example, research has shown that in the first few months, babies seem to relate best to patterns with lots of contrast: stripes, dots, bull's-eyes, and checkerboards. In choosing mobiles and toys, black and white is in, at least as far as babies are concerned. Pastels may be favored by designers and grandmothers, but they appear to be the least favorite colors of tiny babies. Babies do not seem to show a preference for colors until after four months.

A basic principle behind the selection of appropriate toys is called **contingency play**: the best toys are ones where the action of the toy is contingent upon the action of the baby. For example, kicking or batting at a dangling object or shaking a rattle will produce both movement and sound. The baby learns that he has an effect on his surroundings. When playing with your baby, try to set the stage for cause-and-effect actions and reactions. Dangle mobiles (for example, a black and white ball or a paper plate with black and white dots or lines) within striking range and watch how your baby enjoys kicking or batting at them. Rattles, especially ones that strap around baby's wrist so that they can't be dropped, and kick toys (rattles that strap on baby's ankle) are favorites.

Interacting with mom and dad is a kind of contingency play. This is why parents remain babies' favorite toys. When a baby does something that elicits a pleased reaction from his caregiver, this is another kind of cause and effect. Babies seldom get bored with ever-changing human faces. Notice which facial gestures, tones of voice, ways of being held, and toys are pleasing to your baby. Learn what your baby is capable of doing at each stage of development and what he or she seems to like or dislike. This will improve your interactions with your baby and make them more exciting.

Toys and a stimulating environment will never be a substitute for appropriate nurturing. There is no data to suggest that fancy toys make brighter babies. When evaluating how certain toys and certain programs enrich babies, parents as playmates still come out on top. In the keynote address at the 1985 annual meeting of the American Academy of Pediatrics, Dr. Michael Lewis, Director of Child Development at Rutgers Medical School, discussed the effects of early infant stimulation on later outcome. The single most important factor in a child's cognitive development was the mother's responsiveness to the infant's cues. Because of this principle, I often advise expectant fathers to figure out in advance how much money they can afford to spend on toys and baby furniture. I suggest they spend a large portion of this money on their baby's mother instead, to boost her well-being so that she can better nurture their baby.

Baby's Smile Makes It All Worthwhile
Your infant's smile develops in stages. The earliest smiles appear during the first month and are reflex smiles—automatic

facial reactions stimulated by some inner feeling of rightness. They often occur as baby is drifting off to sleep ("sleep grins"). These early smiles convey an "I feel good inside" message. During the second month reflex smiles evolve into response smiles, smiles that respond to some social stimulus, usually a parent's face. These smiles are more defined than the smiles of a newborn. They occur when baby is awake and alert. The whole face is involved, and baby's whole body wriggles along. Smiles are potent activators of adult responses. Babies develop certain behaviors according to their own inner developmental timetables, independent of parents' reactions. But the degree to which a baby practices and refines a skill or behavior depends a great deal on how the parent responds to and reinforces baby's action. When your baby's smile gets a quick and pleasant reaction from you, the reinforcement increases the intensity and duration of the smile. It turns into a smile that involves the whole body: the arms wave, the feet kick, and baby wriggles all over with joy. Your delighted reaction to this smiling body language reinforces the baby's response to your first reaction.

How Babies Move

How your baby uses and moves his various body parts is a fascinating part of infant development. Newborns' bodies tend to be tight. When your baby is lying on his stomach, his legs and arms are drawn up tightly toward his trunk and flexed like a little frog. In the early months his fists are clenched most of the time. When playing with your newborn you will notice that when you pull his arms and legs away from his body or try to open his hands they quickly spring back to their original flexed positions. As the baby matures, you will notice that this spring-like muscle tone becomes more relaxed, as if the baby is gradually unfolding.

Father massage.   Massage can help loosen up the tight two-month-old infant. This is a great activity for fathers and babies. Much attention is placed upon babies' reactions to mothers' bodies, but it is also important that babies get used to a masculine touch.

Place your naked baby on a soft surface in a warm room. Warm a small amount of baby oil in your hands and then stroke your baby's arms, hands, legs, feet, abdomen, back, and head. Stroking from the groin to the foot or from the shoulder to the hand is the best way to relax your baby's limbs. Massage is especially effective in opening the hands. When you massage the back of your baby's hand you will notice his thumb drifting away from his clenched fist and then the fingers beginning, one by one, to unfold from the previously tight fist.

The Third Month: the Payoff

The third month is usually a delightful period for babies and parents. Babies are more alert, active, organized, and responsive. Communication is easier because by this time parents and babies have become comfortable with each other's cues. Mothers and fathers usually describe the third month as easier. You will notice your baby's activity becomes more purposeful, as if he is putting more thought into what he does. The baby's body loosens up, and he assumes an open-arms, open-hands position. In fact, by three months, the baby can

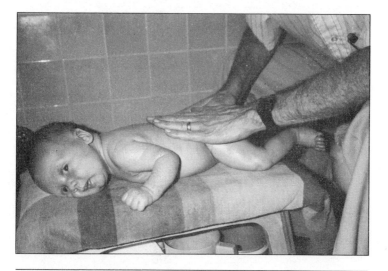

Dad demonstrates the art of baby massage.

Dad Uses Baby Massage

Our first child, Amanda, screamed for hours in the evenings. The most effective method that I could use to calm her was a long walk with her in the Snugli. I liked to do this because not only would she go to sleep, but it gave me some exercise and relaxation.

Our third child, Chelsea, also tends to build up tension during the day and cry unconsolably from about 6-10 PM). A half hour to forty-five minute walk with her in the Snugli usually gets her to sleep at least temporarily.

On a trip to India several years ago, I saw lots of babies who appeared placid and easygoing. I wondered if Indian babies as a group were less fussy than American babies and what might make the difference. Shortly after Chelsea was born, a friend of ours who is a masseuse lent us a book on baby massage combining Indian and Swedish techniques. I decided to experiment with it.

On weekends when I get a chance I give Chelsea a massage. I find that she is too tense and fussy for a massage in the evening, so I do it early in the day, usually before lunch. After a nap she is often in a mellow mood.

I do the massage in the bathroom so I can give her a bath afterwards. First, I draw the bath water and turn on the electric heater for about ten minutes to make sure it's warm enough for her. Almond oil is my favorite for a massage, so I use it for Chelsea also. A small stool that we use for baby changing serves as the massage table.

I start with her feet and legs. Then I do her arms and hands. I massage her abdomen and chest together and, lastly, rub down her back and buttocks. Chelsea then goes into a warm bath to remove the oil and to shampoo her hair. The bath also has a tranquilizing effect on her.

The trickiest part is to take her out of the bath and dress her before she becomes too fussy. This is particularly difficult if the room isn't warm enough or if the new diaper and change of clothes aren't ready. After a massage, she tends to calm down somewhat for the rest of the day. This also gives me a chance to enjoy being with my baby.

finally do something with his hands. Hand play is an important feature of this stage. Baby's fingers fan out and invite you to give him something to play with. Rattles and rings are favorites toys. During the third month, babies also begin to be able to use two skills together to accomplish something. Their vision is quite clear at this age and their hands are open, so naturally they start to use hands and eyes together and begin grabbing for things. Babies love to play with fathers' beards, mustaches, hair, and glasses. Encourage your baby to study and explore your face with his fingers.

Mothers and fathers relate to their babies differently. You will notice that you and your wife play with, talk with, and touch your baby differently. Your baby profits from your unique input.

Three to Six Months

During the first three months, which I call the "fitting-in" stage, your baby acquired two fundamental qualities: behavioral organization and a feeling of trust. If a baby's needs have been met consistently and predictably and his cues read accurately, he fits into his environment and has a feeling of rightness. From this foundation, your baby begins to interact in meaningful ways with his world and his caregivers.

During the previous months you began to feel connected to your baby. Now, after three months, that process has been completed. Your baby at this stage has become highly responsive. You'll see your baby display the same visual and motor skills as in the previous months, but he'll use them for longer periods of time. His hand play, vocalization, and eye contact last longer. He'll be able to engage your attention and entertain you for more than just a few minutes. During the previous stage baby needed to feel that "I fit in." Now it seems that baby is saying, "Because I fit, I'm going to enjoy myself."

Sight and Sound

During the fourth month an important milestone occurs in your baby's visual development—the development of binocular vision, the ability to use both eyes together. Binocular vision enables baby to judge exactly where objects or persons are in relation to himself. By this stage, your baby's eyes can track you a full 180 degrees. Next, you will notice that your baby's head and eyes move together, allowing him to keep a fix on you as you rotate around him.

By the fourth month you may notice that your baby can consistently associate sound with the location of the source. When you enter the room and call your baby's name, baby will turn in the direction of your voice. However, because babies remain primarily visual rather than vocal communicators, it is still a good idea to engage your baby in eye contact before making vocal contact. It is as if your baby is saying, "Look at me when you talk to me."

Reaching and Grasping

Between the third and fourth month baby's visual acuity, head-and-eye movements, and hand play all seem to come together. Increasing hand play is the most interesting motor

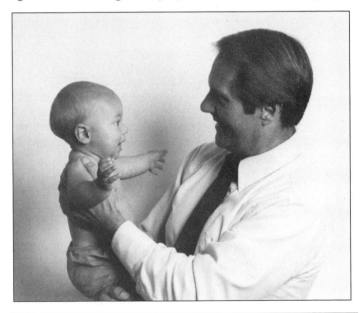

Look into baby's eyes as you talk to him.

milestone of this stage. When he is sitting in his infant seat, baby's hands will usually be together, his fingers interlocking as he folds and unfolds his hands and fingers in self-amusement. For the first time baby can begin to amuse himself for five or ten minute stretches. Babies show great interest in their own intimate space, from their eyes to their outstretched hands. They see clearly at this distance.

Baby's increasing visual ability and hand movements come together in another fascinating ability—visually directed reaching. As a father, I find that one of the most interesting developmental progressions during the first six months is the sequence babies go through in learning to reach out and handle the world around them. In the first three months baby learns to reach out with his eyes. If an object or person sustains his interest, he nods toward the person and his hands wave about aimlessly. During this early stage of reaching, your baby's finger will momentarily point or dart out toward an interesting person or dangling object. This early pointing is the beginning of reaching.

In the first few months baby discovers that his own hands are easily reachable objects and, even more amazingly, part of himself. One hand serves as a target which can be reached and grasped by the other, an important milestone called **hand regard**.

Early on there is very little directionality in baby's swiping and batting at objects, and his misses usually outnumber his hits. Around the third or fourth month baby approaches dangling objects with two hands, a circling and gathering-in variation of reaching. Around the fourth month, baby's reaching takes on direction. In the fifth month baby will reach out with one hand for objects nearly an arm's length away.

From around the fifth month on, baby's reaching takes on fascinating refinements. At first, baby's hand seems to adjust to the shape of the object only *after* it has reached and found it. But slow-motion films of babies' reaching sequences reveal that your baby begins to develop **anticipatory reaching** at this stage. This means that shortly *before* your baby's hand reaches the object, it opens up to accommodate the shape of the object, and the hand slows as it nears the target. In later months baby will begin to make in-flight corrections when the object is moved or the shape of the object he intends to grab is changed. The ability to make special accommodations to the shape and changing distance

---

Dad's Missing Out

I am writing this letter regarding the relationship between my husband and our four-month-old little boy. My concern is that my husband does not spend enough time with our little boy or show him the attention I feel he is wanting from his father. There are times when I am holding our little boy and he will just sit and stare at his father. My husband will turn to him and make noises to get him to laugh or smile but what I would like him to do is pick him up and hold him. I wish he would play with him, have some body contact, and exchange feelings toward one another. My husband will hold him when asked, usually for a short time. We do have another boy who is two-and-a-half years old and my husband helps a lot with him and they spend a lot of time together. My husband really is a wonderful father but his fathering usually starts when they aren't babies anymore. If he only knew all the joy he is missing out on—the loving and comforting feeling you get from holding and cuddling your baby, seeing two little eyes looking into yours sometimes so deeply it's as if you are one, feeling their little hand grasping your finger and holding it tight, hearing the sound of them breathing as they lay on your chest, and just watching them grow and get bigger every day. I am not saying my husband has never experienced some of these things I have mentioned. But he is usually distracted by watching a sports event or something else on TV. There is such a different feeling you can get with your baby when it's just the two of you in a quiet room together. And if he could only experience this and realize that babies are people, too, he would better understand why babies are blessings from God.

of the object reflects the magnificent maturity of baby's visual-motor coordination.

Reaching and grasping used in play. Block play is one of the oldest and best learning tools for a five- to six-month-old. Notice the amazing skills of your baby. He will grasp a block in a mitten-like whole-handed grasp, and then transfer the block from one hand to the other and then from hand

Baby's smiles make it all worthwhile.

to lips. Baby will hold one block in one hand and grab a second block with the other. If you place a third block in front of baby, you encourage him to make a decision as to what he will do with this extra block. Some time around the fifth or sixth month, baby will learn to put one block down to grab the other. Your baby will also begin banging the blocks on the table, fondling them, and turning them over and over from hand to hand, a sign that he is enjoying his newly developed hand skills.

Remember that babies become quickly bored with play activities. In our family we enjoy adding the following activity to block play: place your baby in a high chair next to a table and put three one-inch square blocks on the table within reaching distance on a towel or tablecloth. Use contrasting color blocks or black and white. Station yourself and your wife or a sibling at each end of the table. Pull back and forth on the tablecloth or towel, slowly moving the blocks in front of baby. He will be fascinated by these moving objects and will amaze you with a high percentage of direct hits as his chubby little hands pounce quickly on the moving blocks. Baby's reach and grasp movements during block play are still quick and somewhat jerky as he reaches, paw-like, with his whole hand and rakes the blocks toward him.

When baby is around three months of age, the simplest and most educational toy is a red rubber ring about three to four inches in diameter. A baby can do a lot with this simple, inexpensive toy. He can grab it with one hand, bring it in toward his body, grab it with the other hand, pull on it with both hands, release with one hand while holding on with the other, follow it with his eyes, transfer the ring from one hand to the other, and gum the ring as it inevitably finds its final destination in his mouth. Such a ring is a simple toy that baby can completely control. I have enjoyed many sessions with Matthew playing "grab the ring from daddy." As baby grows and becomes more tenacious, you will have increasing difficulty in getting the ring back.

Open eyes and open hands. Besides using his hands for play, at this stage baby also uses his hands as social signals. By this stage baby is overcoming the tight-fisted posture of the first few months. Now his hands remain partially open most of the time, as if he is inviting you to put something into them. When he is very alert, excited, or interested, his hands are wide open with one or both arms up. You will get the feeling that baby is trying to tell you something with his hands. I call this the **open-eyes, open-hands sign**, baby's invitation for you to come and play. Baby-initiated play has much more learning value and can be sustained for a longer period of time than activity intitiated by you.

Rolling and Climbing
Babies' ability to lift their heads and get their shoulders off the ground develops at this stage, allowing them to enjoy play activity that reinforces these skills. Around five months of age babies love to climb and roll over foam cushions,

Foam cylinders make great climbing toys.

wedges, and cylinders. Pieces of foam from an upholstery shop can be covered with black and white striped material (see photo). Cylindrical foam bolsters, seven to ten inches in diameter and approximately two feet long, make excellent rolling cushions to practice trunk, head, and reaching exercises. It is fun for father to hold baby by the feet and play wheelbarrow. Drape baby over the bolster, and you will notice that he will push himself forward by digging his toes into the carpet and learn to rock back and forth on the cushion using his own foot power.

Six to Nine Months

During the second half of the first year, your baby really starts moving out. The mastering of one primary skill triggers a

---

A Mother's Prayers Were Answered

My prayers regarding the safe arrival of our son were filled with thanks and also the hope that my very busy hardworking husband would become an attentive and active parent.

We had spent the past ten years of marriage just the two of us involved in our business. He had been so occupied with his work that I truly wondered how he would adjust to a baby in our lives.

Well, Benjamin is now five months old and my prayers have been answered. Clyde, my husband, and Benjamin have a wonderful and very intimate relationship. Watching them spend this special time together has given me such joy. It is a blessing to see such a relaxed closeness. They laugh and talk and play like best of friends.

The change in my husband is a miracle for sure. A new part of him has been revealed through the birth of Benjamin. A sensitivity to life that I have only seen occasionally has blossomed and I praise and thank God for our new family.

---

long series of additional accomplishments. Being able to sit without support is a prime developmental skill that opens up a wide new world for baby to explore.

Father's Play Circle
A fun way to play with your baby is to sit baby in front of you along with a few favorite toys and make a circle around him with your legs. This is especially fun between six to nine months when baby is learning to sit up without support. When baby topples backwards or sideways he lands on your legs.

Learning to Crawl
Picture your seven-month-old sitting in the middle of a room a few feet away from various toys just beyond his reach. His intense curiosity and desire to reach his toys, coupled with his increasingly strong arm, chest, and leg muscles, plants the idea in his mind: "I have the capability to reach these toys. Now, how do I get them?" His desire to go forward encourages baby to discover the skills of lengthening and lunging and, eventually, crawling.

The developmental sequence in which your baby progresses from sitting to crawling is one of the most fascinating to witness because there are a lot of different motions involved in this skill. First, baby learns to sit comfortably without support. Next, when you place a toy just beyond his reach you will notice that baby bends his trunk forward as much as possible and stretches his arms and hands toward the desired toy. He'll try to rake the toy toward himself in a paw-like fashion until it is comfortably within his reach and can be manipulated with both hands. If the toy is still beyond his reach, baby begins to fold his outstretched legs in toward himself until his heels touch his diaper. This position allows the baby to rock forward on his tucked-in feet. As baby begins lunging forward on his little rocker bottom, he builds up momentum until the forward movements gradually offset the weight of his bottom and he lurches forward, landing splat on his tummy just short of the wished-for toy.

Undaunted, baby tries to pursue the desired toy by working on the next locomotor skill, crawling.

Babies' early attempts at locomotion are ineffectual and frustrating. A baby's crawling style is as individual as his personality. Babies' first attempts at locomotion are a series of arm, leg, and torso movements which are usually uncoordinated but nevertheless reflect the knowledge that these are their wheels and they have to learn how to roll on them. The arms and legs kick and push in swimming movements that are directed outward from the body, not downward toward the floor. At first, babies are unable to get their tummies off the ground. They may worm their way across the floor in a type of commando crawl, using only their hands and arms, pivoting the upper trunk in circular movements while dragging their hips and legs passively along the floor. Other babies use their legs for propulsion and their arms to steer. It takes varying lengths of time for babies to graduate to a full-fledged crawl, with tummy off the ground and knees and elbows bent.

Baby refines his transportation style by developing the skill of cross-crawling—the arm on the right side coordinates with the leg on the left and vice versa. Baby's head should turn slightly toward the forward hand. If you get down on the floor next to your baby and crawl with him, you will notice that this style of crawling is the most efficient, speedy, and balanced. You'll want to encourage your baby to crawl and develop the correct technique of cross-crawling as this helps develop coordination and provides sensory stimulation to his brain.

Developing locomotion skills not only enables a baby to get from one place to another, it is also an exercise in problem solving, another sign of emerging intelligence. Baby wants a toy that is a few feet away and so he must learn to use his body parts in an efficient way that will enable him to reach that toy. The problem-solving nature of crawling is most noticeable when you place the baby on different surfaces and watch how he adapts his motion to the different textures. When crawling on deep-pile carpet, baby uses primarily his feet and toes to dig in, thrusting forward in a sort of leap-frog style. On the smooth kitchen floor, baby is likely to worm and inch his way across.

Babies love crawling over obstacles. It's fun to play the "crawl over dad" game. Lie down on the floor next to baby and place one of his toys in his line of vision but on the other side of you. This will entice him to crawl over you to reach that toy.

The Pincer Grasp

Crawling is not the only amazing feat that babies accomplish at this age. It is equally fascinating to watch what they learn to do with their hands. They develop the uniquely human capability of using thumb and forefinger together in a pincer grasp.

It is fascinating to watch the sequential development of this skill in your baby. Previously baby raked in objects and grabbed them with his whole hand in paw-like fashion. Gradually baby works his way through the sequential development of the pincer grasp. He has to learn to get the other three fingers out of the way to make room for precise pointing and grasping with his forefinger and thumb. At first, his hands were like mittens; he held a small block between all his fingers and his palm. Next, he holds the object with the index and middle fingers and the palm of his hand, then between the two fingers and the base of the thumb. When he first uses just one finger and the thumb, he'll use the whole index finger until finally, around nine months, he holds objects between the tip of his finger and his thumb in a true pincer grasp.

Putting skills to work.   Once a baby masters a skill he wants to practice it. After he learns to pick up objects with his thumb and forefinger his intense desire to use this skill may overcome his desire to be held. A baby who sees something he wants on the floor will stretch out his hands and squirm in your arms until you put him down to pursue his prey. Gaining the ability to use his arms and legs for locomotion and his hands and fingers for manipulation is not only a major turning point in baby's development, it is also a major turning point in giving mother and father much needed relief from the constant holding and entertaining that most babies need during the first six months. Around seven months, baby is no longer content to be only an in-arms and lap baby; he usually wants *down* so that he can get closer to whatever is interesting on the floor. Babies will often entertain themselves at this stage by sitting and playing with a toy or crawling on the floor toward various enticing objects.

Mothers often complain about their husbands spending too much time with their faces buried in a newspaper. Babies love to sit on daddy's lap and "read" the newspaper. Remember, babies are very interested in looking at things with sharp black-and-white contrasts. Newspaper print fits this description. Don't plan to get much reading done beyond the headlines, since baby will usually bat at, grab, and want to crumple the paper. Wives usually don't complain about husbands spending too much time buried beneath the newspaper when daddy and baby do this together.

Movement as communication.   Besides using his hands and arms for play and movement, baby begins to realize that they can also be used to signal his caregivers. Instead of crying to be picked up, baby will often look up with big eyes and extend his outstretched arms and hands toward daddy in a "please, pick me up" gesture. Respond to these gestures as quickly as you would if baby was crying. This reinforces body language as a means of communication.

Babies are accustomed to mothers promptly responding to their signals. Fathers tend to be more restrained in their reactions, and as a result, babies may not communicate as freely with fathers using hand and eye gestures. Dads can encourage their babies to become equally eager to communicate with them by promptly responding to babies' opening cues, thereby showing baby that they will get the same response from father as they do from mother.

Father Feeding: Starting Solids

Around six months of age most babies are ready to begin solid food. I encourage fathers to withstand the pressure, from yourself and from others to introduce solid foods too early. (Mothers and mothers-in-law are notorious for remarks such as, "Aren't you feeding that baby anything yet?") There was a time when eating lots of solids at three scheduled meals a day and sleeping through the night were seen as evidence of baby's maturity and parents' effectiveness. These ideas have been proven to be untrue. Experts in infant nutrition recommend that solid foods not be introduced prior to four to six months in most babies (or even later in some breastfed babies). Recent research has shown that the infant's intestinal tract is not mature enough to comfortably handle anything but milk before four to six months of age.

Fathers should understand some of the erroneous myths underlying the pressure to start solid foods early. The tendency to space feedings and get babies on schedules is peculiar to western society. It fits in nicely with the idea that women need time away from their babies so that they can pursue more interesting careers. The belief is that if you give baby solids you can space feedings and thus plan for time away from the baby.

More time is spent feeding a baby than in any other interaction during the first six to nine months, and some fathers may feel left out of the relationship between a mother and her breastfed baby. They want to participate in feeding and therefore pressure mother into starting solids early. As I mentioned earlier, the father does have a role in feeding while the baby is still totally breastfed, but this role is to nurture and care for the mother.

Although most babies do not need solid foods for nutritional reasons prior to nine months, most babies from six to nine months are at a developmental stage where they want to experiment with some form of solid food. Babies have the urge to imitate adults in making the food go from plate to mouth. They have the desire to exercise their thumb and forefinger to grasp and pick up small pieces of food, and they also like to begin experimenting with different textures.

Feeding tips. Remember that in the beginning solid foods should complement and not substitute for breastfeeding. Complementing means to add to something. When baby is really hungry, fathers should not offer to feed him solids. It is best to wait until after baby has nursed at the breast before offering solids. Or you can offer solids between breast-feeding times. Breastfed babies are usually hungriest toward the end of the day, a time when mother may be most tired and have the least milk. It is wise to offer solids to the breastfed baby toward late afternoon or early evening. Bottle-fed babies usually like their solids in the morning. If father is the primary feeder of solid food while mother continues breastfeeding, baby is less confused, and the parental roles complement each other just as they do in other areas of child care.

A very ripe banana is a good food to test your baby's readiness for solids. With the tip of your finger place a tiny bit of banana on the tip of your baby's tongue. If he takes the banana into his mouth, he is ready for solids; if the banana comes back at you, baby is not ready. In the first few months babies have a protective tongue-thrusting reflex which causes them to propel anything placed in their mouths right back out. Babies begin to lose this reflex around the fourth to sixth month, and until they do, feeding solids may be unsuccessful, even for fathers. Some babies enjoy it when fathers finger-feed them solid foods. Other babies do not take well to solids unless they can feed themselves. In these babies it is better to place a glob of mashed banana in front of them and let them mess with it a while before trying to get some of the banana from the tray into their mouths.

Self-feeding of solid foods is in keeping with an important developmental and educational principle: a baby is likely to learn more from an activity that he himself initiates. Self-feeding is particularly beneficial to the baby who initially refuses solid foods from a finger or spoon.

Nine to Twelve Months

The end of a baby's first year is often one of the most exciting stages for both father and baby. Once babies can crawl, manipulate objects, and generally *do* more, fathers are more interested in playing with them.

Moving toward Dad

During the first nine months, depending on who is the primary caregiver in the home, babies usually show an obvious preference for mother. But around nine months baby begins periodically to prefer father. Because babies often show an increased interest in fathers toward the end of the first year, fathers often discover that they are more interested in their babies. For most babies, mothers remain the preferred source of comfort, and babies are most likely to turn to mother in times of stress. Books about babies often stereotype parenting roles with mothers being nurturers and fathers being play companions, and babies at the end of the first year seem to agree with this division of labor. Still, I believe that adhering to rigid roles is not desirable for either baby or father (or, for that matter, mother). Even though mother may be regarded as the primary comforter in the house and father as the source of games and play, it is wise for fathers to develop their nurturing role as well.

Learning to Walk

One of the most exciting developments between nine and twelve months is baby's progression from crawling to standing to walking. David, a father who enjoyed his ten-month-old but tended to get bored after ten minutes of play, exclaimed "Finally she can do something and go somewhere!" when his little girl learned to walk.

You'll know that your baby is ready to try walking with your assistance when he starts scaling your pants legs. When you walk into the room your baby will crawl over to you, grab hold of your leg, and pull himself up to a standing position by using your trousers for support. Where previously your baby liked to climb on and over you while you were seated or lying on the floor, now he wants to climb up. To get your attention, he'll chatter away as he comes over and pulls himself up, like a little puppy eager to make contact with his owner. Crawling and scaling open up new social avenues for babies; they can come to you when they need your help or want to play. While I am writing this chapter, I can look down and see eleven-month-old Matthew crawling toward my work table, pulling himself up with the table legs, and pawing along the edge, knowing that something interesting is going on and letting me know that he wants part of the action. If you have been responsive to your baby's cues during the first nine months, your baby will trust you and will now begin to approach you. When I come home from work, Martha says to Matthew, "Daddy's coming home!" He responds by crawling toward the front door and greeting me with the familiar pant-leg pull as if to say, "Glad you're home, Dad. Now let's play."

Babies love to hold onto dad for support while beginning to walk. Begin with the two-handed assist, holding your baby's hands in front of you with both of yours. When your baby masters this skill, progress to the one-handed assist, with baby walking alongside you. Walking with dad is not only a new and fun activity; it also contributes to the development of trust between father and infant. It's the beginning of a long relationship in which the child learns to lean on dad.

The way a tiny baby uses his body for locomotion follows the principles of efficient engineering. Cross-crawling is the most balanced and efficient way to move on hands and knees since one limb on each side of the body is always touching the ground. The way a baby goes from crawling to standing is another developmental marvel. He starts on hands and knees, then bear-crawls on his hands and feet, and then simultaneously pushes up with his hands, lifts his trunk, and throws his bottom back, quickly trying to get his pelvis balanced over his legs. He teeters a bit, then straightens up and off he goes.

Cognitive Development

Around nine months your baby will make great strides in developing the ability to remember, think, and make decisions. He'll learn to find objects that are hidden from view. In earlier stages of your baby's development, out of sight is out of mind. If you hide a toy in your hand, baby acts as

Around one year, baby can follow simple directions.

if the object no longer exists and shows no interest in finding it. Now, however, babies look for toys that have been removed from sight.

Play the game of "Hide the Toy" with your baby: allow baby to watch you hide a favorite object in your hand and then put both hands behind your back. Bring your hands out in front again with the same hand containing the object. Baby will nearly always try to open the hand that he remembers holding the object. Next, try switching the object to the other hand without baby seeing. You will notice that baby still goes to the hand that he remembers held the object. When all he finds is an empty hand, he soon loses interest. Around a year, however, baby's mental abilities have progressed to the point that he will look for the hidden toy in your other hand when the first one comes up empty.

You can play the same game using a toy and two diapers. Allow baby to watch you place a favorite toy under one of two diapers. He will momentarily study the cloth covering the toy, as if he is trying to remember or look for some clue as to which diaper the toy is hidden under. He then makes his decision and pulls off the diaper that was hiding the toy, showing great delight when he makes the right choice. As your baby grows and develops, you can increase the complexity of this game and notice how your baby's cognitive abilities steadily improve.

While these little games may not appear very interesting to adults, they are one way of helping you get to know your baby. Playing simple games with your baby and gradually increasing their complexity helps you know where your baby is at and what he is capable of doing. While baby is growing and developing his skills, you are developing your powers of observation and your ability to understand your baby. This sets the stage for parenting and disciplining your child later on, when a realistic understanding of his capabilities is absolutely necessary. Try to imagine what your baby is thinking based on the way he acts. The ability to get inside your child's mind will help you greatly when problems and confrontations come up later in his development. As in

any business, knowing where you stand at present is necessary to help you plan for and understand the future.

"Daddy and Me" Games for the Nine- to Twelve-Month-Old

Container play. Give baby a clear plastic glass and a small
pellet about the size of a checker (something too large for
him to put in his mouth and swallow). Notice that baby first
uses his pointer finger to feel the pellet. He then picks it up
and with varying degrees of accuracy plops it into the glass.
Taking great delight in his accomplishment (and in the noise),
he then shakes the glass to produce a loud rattling sound.
Once baby masters this feat, he'll keep repeating the sequence of pick up, put in, and shake. This game gives him
the opportunity to make choices and observe their consequences as well as practice his motor skills.

Around one year of age baby can begin to follow your
instructions when playing with blocks and containers. Show
him which block fits through which hole by pointing with your
index finger. Babies are used to following their own pointer
fingers and will, therefore, zero in on yours. Earlier, around
nine months, baby will produce more "misses" than "hits,"
seldom getting the right block through the right hole. But
by twelve months the hits outnumber the misses. Playing with
blocks and containers and matching shapes is not only good
for baby's cognitive skills; it also improves your ability to hold
your baby's attention and get him to follow your instructions.

Block play. Besides the fun of putting blocks into a container and taking them out again, babies love to stack blocks.
Most babies can build a tower three blocks high by the time
they are twelve months old. Block play is another opportunity for baby to practice following instructions. Sit on the floor
facing your baby, or even better, lie down on your stomach
so that your heads are on the same level. I think that babies
get tired of constantly looking up at adults and will maintain eye-to-eye contact better at their own level. Give your

baby instructions such as "Put the block here," and then put the third block on top of the other two blocks. By twelve months some babies can follow instructions closely and will stack the third block or match the right block with the right hole as you direct them.

"Hide and Go Seek." Games you play with your baby should capitalize on the developmental skills attained at a given age. "Hide and Go Seek" does just that. Let your baby chase you around the furniture. Stop and hide behind the couch for a few seconds and then peek around the corner at your baby, saying "Here I am!" This game reinforces your baby's locomotion skills and his memory. He can remember that you went behind the couch, and he can come and chase you out. He may even imitate you by hiding and peeking around the couch himself.

Language games. Even though babies don't say much at this age, they understand more than you might think. Babies can usually understand simple directions such as, "Matthew, get the ball." However, they can't comprehend two things at once, such as "Get the ball and throw it to dad." Give one direction first— "Get the ball"—and after baby has retrieved the ball, add "Throw the ball to daddy." Accompany this last instruction with throwing gestures that will help your baby understand what you mean.

Babies love to imitate and respond to language that is accompanied by gestures, as in the games of "Pat-a-Cake" or "Peek-a-Boo." You'll know that the language is sinking in when your baby completes the pattern of an action after you give him the opening words. For example, after playing many games of "Pat-a-Cake" with your baby, try saying, "Pat-a-cake" without moving your hands. Baby will often take your verbal cue and begin to clap his hands, as if you have touched off a pattern that has been stored in his memory. Be sure, then, to reinforce his gestures by joining in the game.

It's important to keep the game going. Baby reads your cues and responds, you read his cues, and both of you continue the mutual responsiveness. Mothers seem to be better able to pick up on a baby's cues. Perhaps this is because men are too impatient and don't often wait for baby to respond. Harmony at play and mutual responsiveness between father and baby take a while to develop, but you will eventually notice that you are able to hold your baby's attention longer. Don't feel that baby is losing interest in you if he soon loses interest in your game. The average one-year-old seems to have an attention span of less than one minute and then he moves on to something else.

Dads, you may be happy to know that most one-year-old babies can say "Da-da" better than they can say "Momma." Before you let this go to your head, realize that it is also true that many babies say dog (or what sounds like dog) before they say "Da-da."

The more interest you show in your baby now, the more influence you will have on your child later on.

Playing ball. Babies love to pitch a ball and go fetch it. Use a small, hand-size, lightweight plastic ball, like a ping-pong ball. It makes an interesting noise bouncing on a hard floor and moves quickly. Baby can grab hold of it and control it easily. Babies also like large balls that they can hold with two hands. They can imitate a throwing motion by holding the ball with both hands over their heads. But don't expect too many pitches in the strike zone at this age. Babies love it when dads sing to them while playing ball, even if it's just a song you make up.

Roll out the carpet. A play activity which my one-year-old, Matthew, and I have enjoyed is a game I call "roll out the carpet." Get a piece of indoor-outdoor carpet, approximately six by ten feet, (usually available as an inexpensive remnant at a carpet store). Place the rolled-up carpet and a basketful of toys on your patio, porch, or other convenient play area, even a basement or garage in cold or rainy weather. When your baby sees you roll out the carpet and place the basket of toys on it, he will anticipate that this is a special play time with father. This activity capitalizes on two important developmental principles: anticipation and setting the stage. Rolling out the carpet sets the stage so that your baby anticipates play time. Setting the stage for play activities ties in with the basic theme of father nurturing: a child learns to expect that once the stage is set a certain act will follow.

Games Are Important
You may feel that you are just wasting time when you play games like stacking blocks or hiding objects with your baby; you may feel that you should be "doing something" instead. But what seems like meaningless activity to you means a lot to your baby. The more interest you show in your baby early on, the more interest your child will later show in you.

Reference
Hunziker, U. A. and Barr, R. G. Increased carrying reduces infant crying: a randomized controlled trial. *Pediatrics* 77:641-48, 1986.

CHAPTER 6

Nighttime Fathering

Realistically, in most families, nighttime is the only part of the day when fathers and children are at home together. Babies and children get mother exclusively during the daytime and both parents at night. Some get mother both day and night and receive very little fathering at all. Nighttime should be a time for fathers and children to enjoy each other. Fathers can make nighttime into a large quantity of quality time that they can share with their children.

How Babies Sleep

Begin your nighttime fathering career with realistic expectations of how babies sleep—or don't sleep! It's a fact that babies don't sleep through the night. They're not designed to. During the night adults and babies move through cycles of light sleep and deep sleep. Dreams occur during light sleep, and the sleeper seems on the verge of waking up.

During deep sleep the whole body and mind seem to be completely asleep and the sleeper is more difficult to awaken.

Adults experience the whole sleep cycle approximately every hour and a half, moving from deep sleep up into light sleep and back into deep sleep. Around eighty percent of an adult's sleep is spent in deep sleep, twenty percent in light sleep. This means that during an average eight-hour sleep, adults may spend approximately six hours in deep sleep and two hours in light sleep.

By some strange quirk of justice babies are designed with different sleep cycles. Babies experience a much larger percentage of light sleep (around fifty percent), and their sleep cycles are shorter, lasting about sixty minutes. There is a vulnerable period for awakening each time the baby passes from one sleep state into another. This means that babies are biologically programmed to wake up more often than adults.

This hardly seems fair to tired fathers, but let's go back to a basic principle: Babies do what they do because they are designed that way. The ability to awaken easily has survival benefits for the baby. In the first few months of life, babies' needs are great and their ability to take care of themselves is non-existent. Suppose a sleeping baby were hungry and did not awaken. Suppose he was cold and did not awaken to protest. Suppose baby's nose was stuffy and he did not awaken to communicate his need for help. Babies have lots of needs, even at night, and are therefore biologically designed to awaken and communicate these needs.

Some researchers also feel that the predominance of light sleep in tiny babies has developmental benefits (Sears 1985). It is thought that the brain needs exercise in order to develop. During light sleep the brain continues to be active.

Another difference in sleep patterns between babies and adults is the way they fall asleep. Adults can move quickly into the state of deep sleep without passing through a long period of light sleep. In other words, adults can "crash" rather easily. Infants, on the other hand, pass through a period of light sleep lasting around twenty minutes before they enter a period of transitional sleep followed by deep sleep. This has important implications for nighttime parenting. Babies should be parented to sleep, not just put down to sleep. They need to be nursed and gentled through the initial state of light sleep until they are definitely into a deep sleep. Many mothers will tell you that "my baby has to be fully asleep before I can put him down." It is unrealistic to put a tiny baby into a crib, say night-night, turn out the lights, leave the room, and expect the baby to fall asleep on his own and sleep quietly through the night.

You can tell if the baby in your arms is in a deep enough sleep to be put down on the bed without awakening. Signs that the baby is still in a light sleep stage include fluttering eyelids, clenched fists, facial grimaces (also known as sleep grins), and arms drawn up, as if he is trying to hold on to you. A baby in deep sleep, who can be put down gently, has quiet eyelids and facial muscles, open hands, arms dangling at his sides, and generally, a loose feeling. When fathering your baby to sleep, place him down on the bed and gently

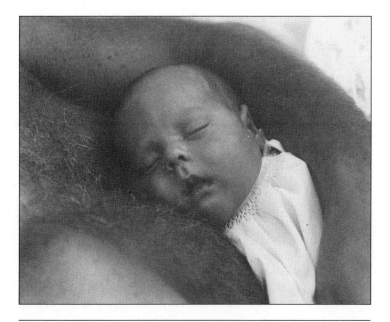

It takes time for babies to fall into a deep sleep.

pat his back at a rate of about sixty beats per minute. Very gradually slow down the motion and reduce the intensity of the pats until the baby is in a sound sleep. As babies mature they are better able to go from being awake directly into the state of deep sleep. Their sleep cycles become longer and the percentage of deep sleep increases. Babies gradually settle more quickly and sleep longer, but they seldom achieve adult sleep patterns until two years of age.

Where Should Babies Sleep?

The goals of effective nighttime parenting are to help babies settle more easily, awaken less fretfully, and develop a healthy attitude toward sleep. Sleep disturbances are common behavioral problems in older children. There are now sleep disorder clinics for children in nearly every major city. I believe that one of the reasons for this epidemic of sleep disturbances is that children have been left to develop unhealthy attitudes toward sleep. Sleep has been a time of loneliness, a fearful time, a time of detachment from known sources of security because children have been put in cribs and left to cry themselves to sleep alone.

Sharing Sleep

Choose a secure sleeping arrangement for your baby. A common question new parents ask is, "Where should our baby sleep?" Let me say right at the outset, whatever way all three of you—mother, father, and baby—sleep best is the right arrangement for your family. In my experience most babies develop the healthiest sleep attitudes when they sleep with their parents in the same bed. I call this arrangement "sharing sleep" rather than the "family bed" because babies and parents share more than just bed space. They also share sleep cycles and probably a lot of as-yet-undiscovered benefits that come from being in close contact with another person at night.

Fathers may regard sharing sleep as both unusual and abnormal. On the other hand, in polling mothers' attitudes on sharing sleep, I have found that the great majority of them feel in their hearts that it is right to sleep with their babies. Many of these mothers, however, choose not to bring their babies into their beds because of pressure from their husbands or from friends and relatives who feel that this sleeping arrangement is unhealthy for the baby and the family.

Shortly after the birth of her first baby, Nancy had read a lot about the advantages of sleeping with babies and had decided to sleep with her new baby. She shared with me her apprehensiveness about her husband's reaction to this idea. She was afraid that he would consider the baby an intruder in their bed and would not agree to the arrangement. When she brought her baby into my office for the one-month checkup she was ecstatic: "He wants to sleep with our baby!" Mothers are overjoyed when their husbands affirm decisions they've made in their hearts.

The emotional and medical advantages of parents sharing sleep with babies are discussed thoroughly in another book in the Growing Family Series, *Nighttime Parenting*. This section is only a brief recap of all the good things that happen when babies and parents sleep in touch with each other. Dads, I sincerely feel that one of the best ways to ensure the development of healthy sleep attitudes in your child is to share sleep with that child when he is a baby.

Easier nighttime nursing. Sharing sleep helps babies and mothers sleep better. During the night babies and parents move in and out of light and deep sleep stages. During the transition from deep to light sleep there is a vulnerable period for night-waking. When mothers and babies sleep nestled side by side they get their sleep cycles in harmony with each other. Mothers wake more easily during the baby's light sleep cycles and sleep more restfully during baby's deep sleep cycles. When baby goes into a vulnerable period for night-waking, mother is also stirring and can nurse the baby through this period without either one waking up completely. When babies and mothers sleep apart from each other, their sleep cycles are out of harmony. Baby often awakens mother out of a deep sleep, and by the time mother gets to baby, both are wide awake. Sharing sleep makes nighttime nursing a lot easier for mom. Not sharing sleep often leads to a tired mother. A tired mother becomes a tired wife and the whole family suffers.

Extra contact for fathers. Besides being good for mothers and babies, sharing sleep benefits fathers, too. A baby needs to grow up with an awareness of the presence of his or her father. Most fathers do not get enough daytime contact with their babies. Sharing sleep with your baby helps you make up for the closeness that you both missed during the day. Sleeping with the baby gives a busy father extra touch-time with his baby.

It usually takes fathers longer to get used to sleeping in the same bed with the baby than it does mothers. Even veteran fathers have spent many nights on the living room couch during those noisy first few weeks or months with baby. Dads, hang in there. You will get accustomed to the baby's normal nighttime noises and will soon be able to sleep through them. I have interviewed many fathers about their feelings about sharing sleep with their babies. The majority of fathers feel a special closeness with their babies because of this sleeping arrangement. Nighttime fathering and sharing sleep allow

"I care" messages to come through all night long, without even saying a word. As a pediatrician I frequently get phone calls in the middle of the night. The disturbance to my sleep is eased somewhat by gazing over at the face of my little sleeping beauty only a few feet away. It is beautiful for a father and baby to awaken and gaze upon each others' faces. Martha and I didn't sleep with our first three babies, but we have enjoyed sharing sleep with our last three. The memories of waking up to the happy faces of my babies will always remain vivid in my mind. I believe that babies also carry with them the memories of waking up in the presence of their fathers, and I suspect that babies who sleep with their fathers will carry this custom into their own fathering in the next generation.

Alternative Sleeping Arrangements
Some babies and parents are too sensitive to each other's presence during the night and do not sleep well in the same bed. Sleep-sharing does not work for all families. Some babies do indeed sleep better with a little space between parents and baby. The sidecar arrangement gives babies and parents individual sleeping spaces but keeps baby close to mother. Remove one side rail from the baby's crib and place the crib adjacent to your bed. Be sure the mattresses are at the same level and fit snugly next to each other so that the baby cannot slip and get caught between them.

If you feel that you cannot sleep well with the baby in your room and choose instead to have baby sleep in another room, here is a tip that will win points for you from both mother and baby: when your baby wakes up at night go and attempt to comfort your baby in the other room and try to resettle him. If nursing is what he really needs, then bring baby in to mother so that she does not have to get out of bed. Mothers whose husbands answer these nighttime calls boast about their husbands' involvement in nighttime parenting. Nighttime fathering seems to earn extra appreciation from mothers, since getting up and tending to baby at night has traditionally been delegated to women. With our first few children I always let my wife answer the distress signals since she had the natural nurturing abilities and equipment for baby-soothing. With our last two babies I have come to feel that perhaps it is a bit unwise for babies to learn to associate only the mother with comfort in times of stress. I have begun to respond to our babies' distress signals. Early on they would greet me with disappointment, as if they had expected mother's soothing voice and warm breast rather than my hairy arms. But the more I attempted to take on the role of back-up baby soother, the more I found that our babies were willing to accept me as a comforter during times of distress. In most instances, however, babies have a strong preference for mother as their primary soother and comforter, at least during the first six months.

Fathering to Sleep

During the first year or two babies much prefer being nursed down to sleep at mother's breast, especially when they have already grown accustomed to this beautiful bedtime ritual. Dads simply cannot and should not attempt to compete with the nursing-down ritual. Babies should go to bed with a tummy full of milk, and mother's milk is the best.

Bedtime Rituals.
After weaning, fathers can take over bedtime rituals. It's only fair that if mothers wake the children up in the morning, fathers should have the job of winding them down at night.

Bedtime stories from daddy.   Recent research suggests that the state of consciousness around the time when a person is falling asleep is a prime time for memory and learning. The next morning, children often remember best what they heard and learned just before drifting off to sleep. For this reason bedtime stories are valuable tools for teaching moral values to children.

Children love bedtime stories about their parents' personal experiences. "Daddy, tell us a story about when you

Baby Misses Dad at Night

I had completely overlooked the possibility that my daughter's disturbed sleep patterns were related to her father beginning a new job and working nights. Everyone was well rested and happy with our family bed until Riana was six months old and Lee had to start a new job. He leaves at 10:30 at night and returns at 7:30 the next morning. Riana's interrupted sleep progressively got worse until one year later I couldn't take any more of her waking every hour to nurse and needing to be comforted back to sleep.

When you first suggested that my husband's leaving at night may be part of the problem, I was reluctant to believe that this could really be the reason for this particular problem. My first thought was, "Well, it shouldn't matter that he's gone. I'm always with her and it's me she wants at night." After some reflective thinking, I said yes this could be it. After all, wasn't it parental bonding that we had worked so hard to achieve? Not just a mother-infant bond but also a father-infant bond. And yes, this problem did really have its beginnings that long ago.

We saw obvious improvements soon after we talked with you. We now talk more about Daddy going to work at night while Mommy and Riana sleep and that Daddy will be home soon after we get up in the morning. We have a very focused family time just before Riana and Mommy go to bed (I make a point to go to bed at her bedtime now and don't leave her.) Daddy tucks us in and helps us say goodnight to the things in our room and he always reassures us that we will all be together again in the morning. Every morning we celebrate his return.

Riana has improved from hourly wakings to sleeping for five hours and waking at two- or three-hour intervals after that. Her naps have increased from twenty minutes to one-and-one-half to two-and-one-half hour stretches. A family bed is Mom, Dad, and baby and when Dad is gone it not only makes Mom uneasy, but baby is unhappy, too.

were a little boy" is a frequent bedtime plea. It seems hard for little children to come to terms with the fact that their parents started out as little children. Children love stories about people they can identify with, and certainly their parents are the people most familiar to them.

The bedtime procrastinator. Ted, a busy father who travels a lot, complained, "It often takes me an hour to put our three-year-old to bed. She keeps nagging for just one more story. I'm tired. She isn't."

Most bedtime procrastinators have fathers who are not around much during the day. Children quickly realize that bedtime is the only time when they have dad all to themselves. Expect your child to use this opportunity to get all the attention he can.

Here is a tip that may shorten the bedtime ritual and help your child fall asleep: agree to lie down on the bed next to your child—with the lights out, of course. I've noticed that our children fall asleep faster when I lie down with them. (A double-sized futon makes this much easier than trying to squeeze into a child-sized bed.) How beautiful it is for a child to go to sleep in the arms of a very important person—dad. The memory will carry over when the child awakes the next morning. This may be especially valuable in families where dad leaves for work before the children are out of bed in the morning.

A bedtime massage. A back rub or soft massage is a very soothing way to father a child to sleep. Using the power of suggestion, tell the child that he's falling asleep as you work your hands down from his head to his feet. Reassure him that you will stay with him until he is asleep. By the time you finish, he'll be sleeping. Fathering your child to sleep, rather than simply putting him to bed, is the real art of nighttime fathering.

CHAPTER 7

Is There Sex after Childbirth?

"I feel left out." "All my wife does is nurse the baby." "We need to get away—alone." "We haven't made love for weeks." "I've got needs, too."

Nearly every father has had these feelings at some time in the first few months after the birth of a baby. Let me assure you that your feelings and your wife's strong attachment to your baby are both very normal.

Why Your Sex Life Isn't the Same

Being aware of the hormonal changes that take place in your wife after birth, and recognizing the importance of mother-infant attachment, may help you understand your wife's apparent lack of interest in sex. Before a woman gives birth, the hormones that influence her sexual behavior are at a fairly high level. After the birth, the pattern changes and the maternal hormones predominate. This situation lasts for at least three to six months and sometimes longer; it may last until the baby is weaned. During this time, your wife's desire to take care of and nurse her baby may take priority over her desire for sexual intimacy with you.

As a survivor of my wife's hormonal changes through six pregnancies and six children, I have developed a theory as to why these changes occur. During my many years as a pediatrician and as a father I have learned not only that babies do what they do because they are designed that way, but also that mothers do what they do because they're designed that way. The shift from attachment to the husband to attachment to the baby seems to be a part of the normal design for the survival of the species. It ensures that the young of the species are well mothered. I explained this all one day to a left-out new father. He commented, "This seems to be part of the for-better-or-for-worse clause in the marriage vows: better for baby, worse for daddy."

Another reason for your wife's apparent sexual disinterest is sheer **fatigue**. Mothers often feel so drained by the incessant demands of the baby and the household that at bedtime all they want to do is sleep. Mothers have described this end-of-the-day feeling as being "all touched out" or "all used up." A mother is programmed to be attached to her baby (your baby) physically, chemically, and emotionally. This does not mean that you are being displaced by your baby, but that some of the energies previously directed toward you are now being directed toward your baby. For the first few months after birth (sometimes longer) most wives do not have the energy to engage in a high level of intimacy both as a mother and as a sexual partner. These energies will eventually be redirected toward you. Meanwhile, you can do something to build up your equity in your wife's sexual interest in you: if you become a supportive and sensitive husband during this early attachment period, your wife's love and respect for you will grow and her interest in you will return at a higher level. This early attachment period is a season of the marriage, a time to parent. If the tasks of the season are carefully tended to, the season to be sexual which will follow will be all the richer.

Rekindling the Sexual Fire

Don't Pressure

Pregnancy, birth, and the early postpartum adjustment period leave a woman physically and emotionally challenged. Let your wife's whole system settle down a while before hinting at sexual demands. As most husbands know, the mental component of sex is much more important in women than it is in men. In women physical and emotional readiness for sex occur together. This is especially true during the postpartum period. A woman's mind is usually not ready for sex until her body is. Many women are truly not ready for sexual intercourse for several months after birth. Pressuring your wife to give too much too soon is doomed to failure. Sex given out of a sense of obligation is not as good as sex motivated by desire.

BABY NEEDS ME, I CAN'T LEAVE HER FOR A MINUTE.

I'M TOO TIRED FOR SEX, I FEEL "TOUCHED OUT."

BUT I'D LIKE TO BE HELD.

I FEEL LEFT OUT.

WE HAVEN'T MADE LOVE FOR WEEKS.

WE NEED TO GET AWAY . . . ALONE.

Communicating needs and feelings will help to restore sexual intimacy after a baby is born.

Go Slowly

Dan, a highly sexual new father, was complaining to his friends that he hadn't had any sex since the baby was born. "The doctor says it's not safe to have sex until six weeks have passed. I can hardly wait." When the sixth week finally arrived Dan made love to his wife, but she at best only passively accommodated him. Their sexual reunion was physically unsatisfying for Dan and emotionally unsatisfying for his wife.

The doctor's idea of when a new mother is ready for sex may be vastly different from when she herself feels ready. After all, the doctor is not the one who is recovering from pregnancy and childbirth while learning to cope with a new baby. Your wife's postpartum checkup is not a green light indicating your sexual relationship can pick up right where it left off.

There is a better way. There is a natural warm-up period that must precede sexual fulfillment after childbirth. A new mother needs to be courted, to be wooed all over again. Most postpartum women respond to a progression very similar to the premarital courtship. Postpartum women want to be held, caressed, looked at, cared for, and loved. For a man, sex equals intercourse. Women, especially postpartum mothers, can experience sexual fulfillment without intercourse. New mothers do feel the necessity to be reconnected sexually to their mates, but sexual intimacy does not return automatically for most new mothers. Many women need a warm-up period of eye-to-eye contact, touching, caressing, and many "I care" messages before sexual intercourse can become fulfilling.

Joan and Larry are an example of new parents going through the process of sexual reunion. Four weeks after the birth of their baby Joan was just beginning to feel sexual urges again. Meanwhile Larry hovered like a sexually thwarted male ready to pounce. When the doctor-prescribed waiting period was over, Larry moved too quickly. Joan stopped him and said "Please hold me for a while instead of making love right away." She needed more time before she felt ready for intercourse.

Go Easy

Respect the physical changes that are going on as your wife's body is returning to its pre-pregnancy state. Some fathers have described their sexual reunions with their wives as "getting to know her body all over again." Sensitivity and gentleness are the keys to fulfilling postpartum sex.

Your wife's breasts may be sensitive because of the changes that occur during lactation. They may leak milk while you are making love so be prepared for this with a towel nearby to catch the drips. Postpartum women may also experience vaginal discomfort or pain during intercourse. The hormones that usually prepare the vagina for intercourse by releasing a protective lubricant are at a lower level during lactation, making vaginal dryness very common in the months after birth. Vaginal pain may also occur if your wife had an episiotomy that is not yet completely healed.

Here are some suggestions to help you and your wife get sexually reacquainted:

1. Make the first night you plan to have intercourse after the birth similar to your first experience of intercourse together—a special time of romance and courtship, complete with flowers and a special dinner. With all the recent changes in your wife's body, you will be getting to know each other all over again. One plus is that "the bulge" is gone, and you'll be able to snuggle close together again.

2. Experiment with positions that do not put pressure on your wife's breasts or episiotomy, for example, the side-lying position. Move slowly and ask her to guide your penetration to avoid pain.

3. If dryness is a problem, use a water-soluble lubricant.

4. Leaking breast milk is a natural part of sex after childbirth. Don't give your wife the message

that this normal bodily function is distasteful. If leaking milk bothers you, having sex after the baby has emptied the breasts may lessen the problem. Don't cry over spilled milk—understand it for what it is: a sign that your wife's body is responding to your lovemaking.

Be Considerate of the Mother-Infant Bond

The feelings of oneness between a mother and her new baby may affect your lovemaking. You may often feel that you are making love to a split personality; mother's body may be in your arms but her mind may be with her baby. Here's the scenario: while you and your wife are making love, your baby cries from another room. (The scent of mother's milk traverses closed doors and thick walls to awaken babies at the most untimely moments.) When this happens, your wife's body and mind respond and she will be more oriented toward comforting baby than satisfying daddy. Fathers, it is impossible to compete with this normal biological programming. Above all, avoid giving your wife the feeling that your baby is spoiling your sexual pleasure. Instead of letting loose with an angry "foiled again" reaction, be sensitive to your wife's biology and to your baby's needs. Say to her, "Go comfort baby first, and we'll make love later." Nothing will earn you more points (and better sex!) than to convey to your wife your understand-

I COME FIRST FOR A WHILE, DAD!

ing that the baby's needs come before yours. A woman is often turned off by selfishness in a man, particularly when it comes to sex. But she will return to your side feeling even more loving and responsive if you have encouraged her to meet baby's needs first. Although you may feel deprived, telling your wife, in words or actions, that the baby has had enough of her attention and that "now it's my turn" is a guaranteed turn-off.

Help Your Wife Find the Time and Energy

Although you may not be able to counteract the natural post-partum changes in your wife's sexual drive, you can do something about the fatigue that may make her feel simply too tired to make love. Take an active part in baby-tending and either share the domestic chores or hire help. One of the best ways to re-direct some of your wife's energy toward you is to pitch in and help with all those household tasks that drain her energy away from your sexual relationship.

Timing is an important consideration in new parents' lovemaking. Time your lovemaking to occur when your wife is the least tired. By bedtime, most new mothers just want to go to sleep. If the baby has been awake and nursing several times during the night, come morning, all mother wants to do is stay asleep. So when do you make love? You'll have to be creative!

For Mothers Only

While it is true that husbands have trouble understanding the sexual changes in their wives after childbirth, it is equally true that wives tend to forget that husbands' sexual urges do not change after birth. Although your hormones change, your husband's do not. Husbands often complain that sex is no longer spontaneous. It has to be planned and scheduled to fit in with the competing demands of another individual in the family. Mothers, remember that for most men sex equals intercourse. While you may need only to be

held and loved, your husband may feel he needs more. To
a man holding and touching may be just a step to go through
on the way to the real thing, orgasm. Let me share with you
some ideas for achieving sexual harmony after birth.

Communicate Your Needs and Feelings

Talk to your husband about your apparent sexual disinterest.
Explain the hormonal changes described earlier in this chapter so that he can understand that you are feeling the way
you do because you are designed that way, not because he
has done anything to turn you off. Be sure he understands
how tired you are. Your husband needs to know that it is
not his fault that sex is not the same after childbirth as it
was before.

Tell your husband what you need. He may be feeling that
you no longer want him because your baby has taken his
place. Let your husband know that you still need him and
that you need and want to be held and touched.

Susan, a woman who worked diligently at becoming both
a giving mother and a giving wife, related the following story
to me. She and her husband were blessed with a baby who
woke frequently at night. Dad, who needed his sleep, moved
out of the bedroom when baby was about one month old
and spent most nights on the living room couch. Recognizing that everyone had nighttime needs, Susan would occasionally tiptoe into the living room and surprise her husband
after the baby had fallen into a deep sleep. These midnight
surprises did wonders to help dad accept Susan's commitment to nighttime mothering. Susan made up for the lost
sleep by napping when the baby slept during the day.

Be Responsive

The number one complaint I receive from frustrated fathers
is, "She doesn't respond to me." When asked about this,
mothers often reply, "I'm too tired" or "I need my sleep more
than he needs sex" or "My baby needs me so much that
I want to save up my energy for her."

Sometimes mothers seem to be physically with their husbands but mentally with their babies, and fathers can sense this detachment. Just as your husband does not expect you to be thinking primarily of him during breastfeeding, neither should you be thinking about your baby during lovemaking. Mothers often have difficulty releasing themselves from the obligations of one role and giving themselves permission to experience the joys of another role. Release, respond, and enjoy your husband. For mother-baby attachment to work in the way it was designed to work, it must be practiced within the structure of a stable and fulfilled marriage. In the attachment style of parenting the whole family works together— mother-baby, father-baby, and husband-wife. Avoid the "but my baby needs me" syndrome. You should not make an either-or choice among these relationships. You need to work at all of them because they complement each other.

The following story is an example of a problem I see in my office all too frequently. Tom and Mary married in their late twenties and had their baby a few years later. Before becoming a mother, Mary had been very successful in her professional career and she wanted to be equally successful as a mother. She decided to stay home, be a full-time mother, and "do it all right." Tom was a bit uncomfortable about handling babies and was more at home on the fast track of his career. Mary sensed Tom's uneasy feelings about his ability to care for the baby and was afraid to leave him alone with the baby. She didn't even trust him to comfort the baby when he cried. As an added stress they were blessed with a baby who had a high level of needs that required a great deal of attachment parenting. Tom felt more and more left out, and gradually they drifted down separate paths, Mary into her mothering and Tom into his work.

Mary became more attached to her baby, and Tom became more attached to his job and also formed a few outside "attachments" of his own. One day Mary was sitting in my office wondering why her marriage was disintegrating. "But I tried to be such a good mother," she said. "My baby

needed me. I thought Tom was a big boy and could take care
of himself."

Mothers, watch out for "red flags" in your family. Are there
problems in your marriage? Is dad enjoying his work more
and his home less? I told Mary that "what your baby needs
most is two parents." Tom needed more of her attention and
her trust, and the two of them needed to decide together
how they could take care of each other's needs as well as
the baby's. With better communication and some give-and-
take, they managed to work things out. Both of them matured as parents and as spouses.

Maturing as a Father—Maturing as a Man

What's in it for dads? Nothing matures a man more than
fathering a new baby. An important part of becoming a mature person is being able to give part of yourself to someone else. Another part of growing up is learning to delay
your own desires in order to answer a need that someone
else has.

New fathers go through a kind of second adolescence.
Adolescents are naturally impulsive but must learn that it
is often wise to delay the gratification of impulses. You may
feel that you want to get away alone with your wife and that
the baby always wants her when you want her. You realize
that you must now share your mate with another person. Handling these feelings can have a maturing effect on a man.
Remember that during the first year most of what a baby
demands from parents is simply what he or she needs.
Resenting your baby for taking your wife away from you or
resenting your wife for putting the baby's needs first can stand
in the way of becoming a giving father. It can also greatly
diminish the joys of being a parent. Fatherhood is one big
give-athon. The earlier we learn to give, the greater the joy
in becoming a father.

Fathers who have felt that they suffered from an acute
lack of sex in the first few months after birth but who have

developed the maturity to accept delayed gratification of their needs often find that their overall relationship with their mate improves. Understanding and respecting the natural design in the first few months after birth forces the husband to seek ways of achieving sexual intimacy with his wife outside of intercourse. In ancient times writers about sex described the sexual relationship as "to know" another person. While this can be interpreted specifically to mean sexual intercourse, I believe the phrase "to know" conveys many other levels of meaning as well. It describes the mutual adjustments that a couple make when they become parents. By understanding that a sexual relationship involves more than intercourse, the husband truly gets to know his wife. Yes, there is sex after birth! It is a fuller and richer kind of sex that matures a man as a male person, a husband, and a father.

CHAPTER 8

Fathering the High Need Child

Some babies and children are more challenging than others. You may be blessed with a special type of baby who is known by various descriptive labels—fussy, exhausting, demanding, colicky. As these babies grow older they acquire additional labels, such as "hyperactive" or "strong-willed." I prefer to call this kind of child a "high need child." This is not only a kinder term, but it is also more accurate. It describes what these children are like and suggests something about the kind of parenting they need. High need babies can put a severe strain on families if their needs are not recognized and responded to sympathetically. They require a great deal of parenting energy, but the investment-return ratio is high. The more you can give to this type of child the more you and the rest of the family will get back in return. "I could not have survived without the help of my husband," confided Joan, a tired but fulfilled mother of a high need baby.

Recognizing the High Need Baby

High need babies are not hard to recognize, even when they are very small. They share certain personality traits, and they let you know early on that they will not compromise when it comes to having their needs met. Here are some of the ways parents have described their high need children.

Intense
High need babies put a lot of energy into their behavior. They cry loudly; they laugh with gusto; they seem as though they are always in high gear. Their attachment to their parents is strong, and they are quick to protest when they're separated or when their needs are not met promptly.

Super-Sensitive
High need babies have short fuses. They are easily bothered. They startle easily and take a long time to settle down. High need babies are keenly aware of changes in their environment and do not adapt easily. All babies come endowed with stimulus barriers that allow them to filter out disturbing signals from their environment; high need babies have less selective stimulus barriers. They startle easily during the day and are difficult to settle at night. These babies trust in their parents to provide the security and the protection from over-stimulation that they cannot provide for themselves.

Active
High need babies are very physically active. They never stop moving. As one photographer-father described his baby, "There's no such thing as a still-shot." Another father said, "His motor seems stuck in fast idle."

In-Arms
"I can't put him down, he wants to be held all the time" is a typical description of a high need baby. These babies crave physical contact. They have difficulty relaxing by themselves, and they certainly are not noted for their self-soothing

abilities. Many new parents expect their babies to lie quietly in their cribs, gazing serenely at a dangling mobile. Few babies live up to these expectations, and this is certainly not what you can expect of high need babies. They prefer to be in a parent's arms or at mother's breast.

Draining
High need babies wear out their caregivers. At the end of the day when you have long been ready to crash, these babies are still revved up and going strong.

Wakefulness
A tired father once lamented, "Why do high need babies need more of everything but sleep?" The sensitive temperaments of high need babies don't shut down at night. These babies are highly alert and are often described as "tiring but bright." The brightness can last all night long, as if they are lit by an internal light bulb with a hard-to-find off-switch. This brightness can keep high need babies—and their parents—awake at night.

Unpredictable
No one thing works consistently to comfort these babies. Just when you think you've got the game figured out, the baby changes the rules. As one father put it, "Just when I think I have the game won, she ups the ante."

Frequent Feeders
The term feeding schedule is not in the vocabulary of high need babies. They have a great need for sucking and nurse often for comfort as well as nourishment. They also generally need to nurse longer and are slow to wean. It is not unusual for high need babies to nurse well into the third year.

Uncuddly
While most babies melt into the arms and chests of their parents, high need babies may stiffen, arch their backs, and pull away from parents' bodies, even while they insist on

being held. This is a tough character trait to become accustomed to because it violates parents' natural expectations that babies who want to be held will stay calm as long as they are held. Uncuddliness can be devastating to a mother especially; she may feel that she is not getting through to her baby because she does not get the positive feedback that comes from the baby nestling quietly and securely into her arms. Parenting begins to seem like "all give and no get."

Demanding
Being demanding is the number one character trait of high need babies. There is a sense of urgency in every one of their signals. Almost every cry is a red-alert. They do not know the meaning of delayed gratification and are quick to protest if their cues have been misread and the wrong solution is offered.

The Positive Side
This profile of a high need baby may sound predominantly negative. This is how parents perceive these babies early on. I have observed, however, that sensitive parenting can turn these seemingly negative traits into more positive ones. Parents gradually begin to describe their high need children in more positive ways: challenging, interesting, and bright.

The intent of this chapter is to help fathers turn the difficult qualities into creative assets. Fathers have an important role to play in parenting the high need child. They can help in three ways: by interacting with the baby, by supporting the mother, and by improving their own sensitivity.

Understanding High Need Babies and Their Mothers

A high need baby can create a lot of stress in a marriage. One disappointed and confused new father said, "Our baby brings out the best and the worst in us." There are many reasons why high need babies strain the marital relationship. The baby you imagined when your wife was pregnant was probably cute and cuddly and easy to take care of. The baby you got turned out to be demanding and challenging and fussy. The long-awaited asset seems to be a big liability. You probably didn't realize during your wife's pregnancy how much a new baby would dominate your lifestyle. You were not prepared for a baby who would drain away all of your wife's energy—energy which had previously been directed towards you and towards the marriage. On top of all this, your baby may have such a strong preference for mother that he has difficulty relating or responding to you at all.

Some fathers deal with the challenges of a high need baby by escaping. Instead of sharing the parenting responsibilities with their wives, they bury themselves in their work and drift into other outside commitments. It may be difficult to understand why high need babies—and their mothers— behave the way they do, but it is the first step toward becoming an effective father to your high need child. It will also pay off in an improved relationship with your wife.

The Need-Level Concept
Every baby has a distinct temperament that is determined primarily by genetics. By temperament, I mean simply the

DAD, I'LL BRING OUT
THE BEST IN YOU.

way that a child behaves, how he communicates, how he reacts to the world around him, his style. Babies also have different levels of needs. They have an intense desire to fit into their environment, but some need more help than others in order to achieve a good fit. High need babies have a hard time fitting in. They need lots of care and attention from parents to help them fit. Fortunately, they come endowed with temperaments that ensure that they get the attention they need.

Babies' behaviors communicate their needs. For example a baby who very much needs to be held in order to feel that he fits will cry intensely until he is picked up and will start crying again if he is put down. Babies don't cry in order to annoy, manipulate, or make their parents miserable. They cry to communicate their needs. Babies with greater needs give more intense cues. This is why high need babies are often labeled as "demanding." Being demanding is a positive character trait that helps your baby reach his or her maximum developmental potential. If your baby had great needs yet lacked the ability and the determination to communicate those needs, he would not receive the help he needs to fit into his environment. His developmental potential would be threatened because he would not learn to trust himself or the people around him. He could not develop a sense of competence and self-esteem. Babies do what they do because they are designed that way. Respecting that design ensures that the baby will develop his full potential and that you will develop into an effective, sensitive parent.

Fathering the High Need Child

How you father your high need baby affects two people— your baby and your baby's mother. Your wife needs your psychological support and your readiness to fill in as "mother" when she has run out of steam. Here are some tips that will help you make things easier for the two most important people in your life.

Positive Feedback

Reassure your wife that your baby's behavior is *not her fault.* Mothers naturally take their babies' behavior personally. Because she feels that her baby is an intimate part of her, your wife takes both the credit and the blame for the baby's positive and negative traits. Comments from other parents or from outside advisors contribute to these feelings of self-blame. Mothers of high need babies are bombarded with guilt-inspiring admonitions:

> "Maybe it's your milk."
> "You're holding him too much. You're spoiling him."
> "If you'd let her cry a while, she'd learn to settle herself."

You can counteract the effects of outsiders' comments by giving your wife lots of positive feedback about her mothering style.

Another factor that contributes to a mother's guilt feelings is comparisons between her baby's behavior and that of other babies. The baby's behavior becomes a measure of the mother's effectiveness. This standard couldn't be more wrong. When they talk to others, mothers often exaggerate the "goodness" of their babies in order to subconsciously reinforce their own estimation of their effectiveness: "My six-week-old baby sleeps through the night, and I can leave her with anyone." Your wife is forced to conclude that she must be doing something wrong; otherwise her baby would be acting as contented as the baby next door.

Dads, remember that parenting is inherently a guilt-producing profession. Love for another human being makes you vulnerable to any suggestion that implies that you may not be doing the best you can for that other person. Remind your wife frequently that your baby acts the way he or she does because this is his nature; it isn't the result of anything mother is doing or failing to do. Your wife needs lots of reassurance from you because she is probably not getting it from her friends or from her interaction with the baby.

Be Upbeat!

It is very natural for your wife to feel progressively more down in the dumps when all she hears from her friends are negative comments and her baby seems to be constantly unhappy. Stress the uniqueness of your baby, not the difficulties. Use uplifting terms to describe your baby, such as spirited, challenging, bright, stimulating, never dull.

Acting upbeat when you yourself feel tired is very difficult for dads or for anybody. But your feelings and behavior make a tremendous difference. Debbie, an exhausted mother of a high need child, confided, "When I'm down, my husband is up and that is what keeps me going. If we were both down at the same time I don't think we'd survive." If your wife senses that you have negative feelings about your baby's behavior, it reinforces her feelings that the baby's behavior is her fault. By disapproving of your baby, you are also giving your wife the message that you disapprove of her mothering and, therefore, of her. Many mothers derive a lot of their self-esteem from how their husbands perceive their mothering abilities. We all need strokes, especially mothers of high need babies.

Seek Outside Support

How can you keep your own outlook positive while you help boost your wife's feelings? Surround yourselves with supportive friends. Nothing divides people like differing views in child-rearing. Protect your wife from these negative advisors by purposefully seeking out friends who share your own parenting styles and who can be supportive of you rather than critical.

Hire help at home or pitch in yourself in order to free your wife of non-mothering chores which divert her energy away from the baby (and also away from you).

Be Involved

Eric, a mathematician and involved father of a high need baby, felt that most problems had mathematical answers. He summed up his solution, "Our baby has two mothers, the milk mother and the hairy mother."

Shared-parenting is not only desirable for the high need child, it is absolutely necessary. Take over when times get tough. Fussy babies usually save their most exhausting behavior for the end of the day, between 4:00 and 6:00 PM, when mothers' energy reserves are at their lowest. It's sort of a "happy hour" for babies, but a few cocktails are not the answer. If you come home from work at the end of the day and your castle, queen, and little princess are all a wreck,

Sometimes dad's strong arms can soothe a
fussy baby after mom's arms give out.

it's not a good time to express your disappointment. Instead, say to your wife, "You take a nap or do something just for yourself, and I'll take over with baby." (And then send out for pizza!)

Sometimes a change in comforting persons is all that a fussy baby needs. Other times you'll need to have more tricks up your sleeve. Here are some tips especially for fathers.

Freeway fathering. Fussy babies often quiet down when they are secured safely in a car seat and lulled to sleep by the motion and sound of the car. When you return home and baby is in a deep sleep, don't risk waking him by removing him from the seat. Instead, carry baby, car seat and all, into the house to continue his nap.

Holding patterns. High need babies need frequent changes in how they are held. You'll need to invent different ways to hold your baby next to your body. Fathers are more than substitute mothers when it comes to carrying their babies. They have unique techniques that can calm even the fussiest of infants. See Chapter 5 for suggestions.

Dad Wants to Help More

I have been experiencing some frustration lately over my inability to relieve some of the pressure my wife is feeling in caring for our new baby. We are coming to realize that we have been, as you so appropriately put it, blessed with a high need child. Our son has a high need to be held and have close contact. He does not enjoy being left in his swing or laid in his crib for any length of time. What frustrates me is I cannot comfort him as my wife can. I want to help her out, and I want to feel that I can meet my child's needs, but a lot of the time there is nothing I can do to calm him and he isn't happy until he is back in mom's arms. This leaves me feeling bad because I can't give my wife the break she needs and I can't spend time with my son.

There may be times when a baby simply wants and needs to be put down on a soft carpet and allowed to blow off steam. Sometimes fathers are better at recognizing these times than mothers. Your wife's natural reaction to the baby's signs of distress is either holding or nursing, and most of the time these do the job. But sometimes it takes a suggestion from father to find the way to calm a fussy baby: "Maybe she needs to exercise to blow off a little steam. I'll sit here with her for a while so you can take a break." When you offer advice to your wife about baby care, focus on what you feel the baby needs at that moment, not on what you feel your wife ought to be doing. Remember that your wife often feels that her baby is acting the way he does because of something she is doing wrong.

Don't Pressure Your Wife to "Get Away"
Fathering a high need child often reminds me of the advice the famous Notre Dame football coach Knute Rockne gave to his players, "When the going gets tough, the tough get going." In other words, tough guys hang in there rather than trying to escape. Some fathers tend to want to escape periodically from their babies because they are tired of competing for intimate time with their wives. But this is seldom the ideal solution to the problem.

Dan and Susan were exhausted parents of Jessica, a three-month-old high need baby girl. Susan was struggling but managing to meet Jessica's needs and even have a bit of energy left over for herself and her relationship with Dan. Dan felt a bit left out, and he frequently imagined a romantic escape from parenting in which he whisked his wife away to a romantic island to rekindle the flame of their earlier relationship.

One day Dan had a chance to close a big business deal on the other side of the country, and since he figured it was time he and Susan got away alone, he pressured her to come with him and leave Jessica behind (and to consider weaning her, too). Dan also felt that Susan would be an asset in closing the deal. Susan shared her dilemma with me. She felt that she was put in a no-win situation. One side of her wanted to get away with Dan, but her maternal instincts told her that Jessica was not ready to be left with someone else. I suggested to Dan that this no-win situation extended to the entire family: Susan would probably not be the relaxed and romantic mate he wanted with him on his trip, and Jessica would be more difficult to handle if she was weaned before she was ready. I convinced Dan that pressuring a mother to go against the desires of her heart is doomed to failure.

The solution? Dan, Susan, and Jessica took off for New York together. Jessica nursed all the way, coast to coast. Dan was overjoyed to discover that his business contact had also brought his wife and baby along. In fact, the wife exclaimed, "I'm so happy you brought your baby along, too. We have one of those babies who just can't be left." The two fathers felt a kinship because they both placed high priority on their families. The business deal was closed successfully.

Preventing Mother Burnout

Burnout is a common disease among modern mothers. It is usually the result of a dedicated mother trying to do too much for too many with too little help. Burnout is not a disease of the weak; it is a disease of the strong and is most common in mothers who are committed to doing the job right. You have to be on fire before you can burn out. Burnout, like many diseases, is preventable, and the primary means of prevention is an active, involved father.

Mothers of high need babies are at a higher risk for burnout. Babies have a way of extracting large amounts of energy from their mothers. Mothers in turn are programmed to be giving and nurturing and to supply all the energy demanded by the baby. This is nature's way of ensuring the survival of the young of the species. Mothers keep giving as babies keep demanding, sometimes to the point where mothers lose touch with their own needs and fail to realize that they are giving out. The mother is programmed to fill her baby's needs, but who takes care of the mother's needs? That's where father comes in. In the family with a high need child, fathers must help balance the needs equation. They do this by giving to both mother and baby and by helping the mother realize her own limitations.

Recognizing the Early Signs of Burnout

While mothers are noted for their untiring energy, fathers are equally notorious for their inability to recognize when a mother is at the end of her rope. A stressed-out mother of a high need baby once confided to me, "I'd have to hit my husband over the head before he'd realize that I'm giving out." Mothers do not want to appear weak in the eyes of their husbands. Therefore even if they recognize early symptoms of burnout in themselves, they may fail to share these symptoms with their husbands. It's up to you as a father to recognize the symptoms of impending burnout.

Mother burnout often carries over into the marriage. A burned-out mother becomes a burned-out wife. A woman who feels inadequate as a mother will often feel inadequate as a person, too. Fathers have a strong interest in preventing maternal burnout, since it can quickly become a problem for the whole family.

Risk factors. Certain mothers of high need children are at higher risk for burnout.

1. Women who were involved in high-profile careers before becoming full-time mothers.

2. Mothers of babies who are close in age, that is, less than two years apart.

3. Highly motivated and compulsive mothers.

4. Women who experienced a stressful labor and delivery or who were separated from their babies after birth because of medical problems.

5. Mothers who live in busy nests because of remodeling, moving, social commitments, too many visitors.

6. Mothers experiencing marital discord, especially those who believe (unrealistically) that a baby will solve the problems in the marriage.

Signs and symptoms. One of the earliest signs of mother burnout is when your wife begins to feel that she is not a good mother. She may also stop taking care of herself and pay less and less attention to her grooming, unknowingly making herself less attractive to you. She excuses this by saying, "My baby needs me, I don't have time for anything else." What energy she has goes to the baby, with little left over for herself and none at all left for you. Mothers nearing burnout tend to make mountains out of mole hills. They are

NAME *MRS. BURNED OUT*

℞ *1 DOSE OF CARING HUSBAND 3 TIMES A DAY, UNTIL SYMPTOMS SUBSIDE.*

REFILLS *AS NEEDED.*

WM. P. Sears, M.D.

confused by the slightest setback and tend to jump all over their husbands with very little provocation. Burned-out mothers often quit exercising and suffer insomnia.

It can be hard to get through to the burning-out mother. You need tact and the right angle on the problem. Instead of focusing on what's best for the mother or on what you need, focus on what's best for the baby. Mothers respond to this approach because they are naturally oriented to think of the baby first. Convince your wife that taking better care of herself will benefit the baby. Some mothers actually need permission to release themselves temporarily from their obligations to their babies, and the father is naturally in a good position to grant this. Don't allow your wife any room for excuses, because she will certainly find them if they're there. Present her with definite plans for some time to herself: a gift certificate for an hour or two at a spa or beauty parlor; an invitation for lunch at a friend's house; a gift certificate for a shopping trip; a promise from you to take care of the baby (in some far corner of the house) while she spends an uninterrupted hour at a favorite hobby or with a book.

What's in It for Dads

Believe it or not, there are advantages to having a high need child. You've heard that it takes two adults to make a baby. A high need baby will turn you and your wife into bona fide adults, capable of greater amounts of selfless giving than you would have thought possible.

Many mothers are justified in their unwillingness to let fathers care for the baby because these fathers have not demonstrated that they are capable of comforting the baby. Fathers must earn this trust. If you have been consistently involved in your baby's care from early on, your wife will learn to trust your ability. When your wife trusts and respects you as the involved father of her child, she also respects you more as a man. Being sensitive and caring for your wife when she is down and discouraged will earn you a lot of love and respect. One of the greatest ways to increase your wife's love for you is to love her child. Sharing in the care of your high need child benefits your marriage.

The experience of having a high need baby matures a father. It brings him out of himself and teaches him more about caring for another person. A father of a high need baby also learns to be a skillful father, especially in the art of comforting a fussy baby, a task that has traditionally been left to mothers. Fathers of high need babies often report that they know their child well and feel very close to their child as a result of all the contact they've shared.

Martha and I have been blessed with one high need baby out of our six children, our daughter Hayden who is now an eight-year-old high need child. Her needs don't lessen with time; they only change. During her first two years of life, Hayden required every bit of parenting energy we could muster. It was not until several years later that I realized how much she gave back to me as a father. I truly feel that I am now begining to cash in on my early investment in her.

Over the years, I've talked with the parents of many high need babies. Some of their experiences have had good outcomes, some not so good. Do you know what I discovered in searching for the differences between the good experiences and the poor ones? The most important difference was not whether the baby was breastfed, whether his cries were promptly responded to, whether the baby slept with the parents, or even whether the baby was cared for by a full-time mother. The high need babies who grew up to have the most self-esteem and who brought the most joy to their parents had one thing in common: a caring and involved father.

CHAPTER 9

Solo Fathering

There was a time when mother's and father's roles were strictly defined. Mom kept house and tended babies; father was the breadwinner and usually worked away from the home. For better or for worse, these roles are no longer strictly defined. The social forces that have taken mothers out of the home have forced fathers to be more involved at home. The term homemaker can now be said to apply to both mother and father.

Father as a Baby-Sitter

I don't like the term baby-sitter, especially when applied to fathers. It implies that dad is just filling time until mother returns and is not interacting with the baby. Let's call it solo fathering instead. After all, the father is not just a substitute mother; he has his own unique contribution to make to his child's development.

The time when mom's away is your chance to really shine. Being alone with your baby gives you the opportunity to be totally yourself and forces you to be a creative entertainer and comforter since mother is not there to bail you out. When there's only baby and you, that's a special time. Here are some suggestions to help you and your baby enjoy this special time together.

Be sure mom leaves baby well-fed.   If your baby is breast-feeding and is too young and too smart to accept any substitute form of nourishment, insist that your wife leave the baby with a full tummy. If your baby will accept substitute feedings, be sure mom leaves a back-up bottle, preferably filled with expressed breast milk. Remember that sometimes fathers need to be more creative in comforting babies than

mothers are. Breastfeeding mothers can usually rely on that favorite of all pacifiers, the breast. Fathers can't.

Plan ahead. "Maximize your time" is a catch phrase of time-management advisers. Many fathers spend much of their business day planning how to get the most out of a little time. The same goes for solo fathering. Try to get your non-fathering obligations out of the way so that you are all there— body and mind—when you are with your baby.

You might even plan the activities you are going to do with your child, bearing in mind that babies may not always be in the mood to play the games you have chosen. It is easy to entertain the older child; the decision is usually as simple as which kind of ball to play with. Entertaining babies and toddlers requires much more ingenuity.

Mothers often try to leave babies with their fathers during naptime, hoping that the baby will sleep until mother returns. While this may be wise to do with a tiny breastfeeding baby who sleeps an hour or two at a stretch, it may not always work and it then leaves father in a difficult spot. When babies wake up prematurely from their naps, they usually feel very unsettled and need to go back to sleep. It is usually difficult for fathers to re-settle them without mother being there to nurse them back to sleep. For some babies a better time for solo fathering is just after they wake up and are well rested.

Get on your baby's own level. It's challenging and fun to try to figure out what a baby is thinking and feeling by the way he looks and acts. Mothers seem intuitively able to see the world from baby's viewpoint, but this can be hard for fathers to do. Make it a game you play with yourself: "I wonder what baby's thinking now." Getting on the baby's wavelength means you have to stop worrying about potential problems (What happens if he gets hungry? What if he has one of those explosive bowel movements where he needs a bath as well as a diaper change?) and really focus on the baby. Feel confident in yourself so that the baby will feel confident with you.

Uniquely dad games. While you are solo fathering engage baby in activities that are different from how the two of you play together when mom's around. Saving special play for these special times makes it easier for babies and children to accept solo fathering, especially during the first year when babies are very sensitive to mother's absence.

Fathers Need to Be in Charge

My recommendation is that father insist on taking over regularly, not wait until mother has had it. By taking over I mean as completely and for as long as possible, e.g., after the child is weaned, it could be for a whole day. To the extent feasible, there should be no possibility for father to bail out. Let mother enjoy an unencumbered day of creature comforts.

The benefits are manifold. Mother will love you for it, and will run out of physical and emotional energy far less frequently. An hour, a morning, or a day of peace is a wonderful, renewing thing.

A father will never know his child fully until he has had sole responsibility for decision-making: does he need a diaper change? is she hungry? does he need a cuddle? is he cold? etc? Becoming sensitive to your child's signals depends on your need to do so. You cannot perfect your cooking skills by watching somebody else cook— and you'll never perfect your parenting ability by watching mother parent. Having sole responsibility for my children has been one of the most rewarding and enjoyable experiences of my life.

Father and children will invariably grow closer, as they become more aware of and sensitive to each other's feelings. Also, father and mother will both find comfort in knowing that in the event of emergencies, father can confidently and effectively care for the children.

It's a real winning situation for father, mother, and children.

From around nine months to one year of age, babies love games that are variations on peek-a-boo. The two of you can chase each other around the couch singing "Where's daddy?" Bob up and down periodically to reveal yourself and say "Here I am." Look for the surprised expression on baby's face and approving chuckles. If you get these responses, continue playing, but remember that babies get bored easily. If you don't get an approving response to your game, don't persist. Change games.

Between six and eighteen months babies love to climb all over you because you are like a moving jungle gym. Climbing on someone is better than climbing on something because the someone moves and gives baby some feedback about his efforts. When your baby climbs onto your chest and you pick him up over your head to play "flying baby," you are rewarding him for initiating the climbing. Mothers tend to play quieter, less active games with babies. They focus their play activities in a small area, and babies learn to accommodate these limits. Fathers widen baby's playtime interests with more vigorous climbing and tumbling play. Many dads have trouble sitting still in one place and concentrating on a narrow play activity. They need space and so they naturally use more space when they play. Babies profit from exposure to these bigger play areas.

Special safety awareness.   Accidents may occur more readily when father is minding the store. I do not mean to imply that fathers are careless, but fathers may not be completely aware of babies' impulsive behaviors and capabilities at a given stage of development. Sometimes I wonder if mothers really do have eyes in the backs of their heads, along with third arms and radar systems that pick up on babies' collisions with furniture before they occur. Fathers need to be aware that since they are new to the job of safety patrolling, they need to be extra cautious in leaving baby unattended. You may be very tired, but resist the urge to take a nap while solo fathering. Mothers seem to have a heightened awareness of their babies even during sleep, but fathers usually don't. While this ability to tune out babies' cries can be an asset during nighttime co-parenting, it is a liability during solo fathering.

Be consistent and predictable. If both you and your wife have practiced the attachment style of parenting which I advocate throughout this book, your baby has developed trust in you and is accustomed to receiving a response in answer to his cues. It is not important that you respond in the same way that your wife does; after all, you are not the same person. But it is important to the baby's feelings of self-esteem that he gets the sort of response he has learned to anticipate. For example, a baby who has learned to trust his parents expects that distress will be followed by comfort. Your

---

Dad Takes His Turn

The other evening my husband announced he was taking Kristen, our five-month-old daughter, down to the beach to see the sunset. Normally, I would get myself ready and go along, but I was in the middle of fixing dinner and couldn't get away. I had a feeling, too, that maybe this was one time when I should stay home.

I said good-bye to the two of them as they went out the door together. Something about the way he marched off with her told me daddy was enjoying this—and was probably glad mommy wasn't coming along.

I watched from the window as he put her in the car seat and drove off, feeling a little nervous. Now I have left Kristen home with Ron for short periods while I went out, but this was different. My instincts told me it was important for Ron to have this time with her without me hovering nearby reminding him to be careful about this and don't do that. This was different from baby-sitting at home for an hour. This was being actively involved and responsible, and, in spite of my initial hesitation, I was truly overjoyed to see it happening.

---

method of comforting a crying baby may be different from your wife's, but it's important that you do respond to your baby's cries. A time when you are solo fathering is not the time to let the baby "cry it out." This is not likely to make baby look forward to times alone with you. But practicing attachment fathering will.

Be trustworthy. Not only is it important that your baby trust you, but it is also important that your wife trust your abilities in solo fathering. Most mothers have difficulty releasing their baby to anyone else's substitute care—even to the baby's father. Your wife will be able to enjoy her time away from the baby only if she trusts your willingness and ability to be a caregiver. You can't fool mothers. When they return home, they have a way of sensing whether or not their babies have been given the proper care. You may be surprised at how good your wife will be to you if you have been good to her baby. While talking with parents in my office I am impressed by an admiring sparkle in a mother's eye when she looks at her husband and says, "He and our baby have a very special relationship while I'm away."

Fathers and the Working Mother

The issue is not the working mother. The issue is being away from the baby. Mothers have always worked, in all cultures, inside and outside of the home, but they worked without leaving their babies. The new issue today is that mothers are working in one place while babies are cared for in another. This puts a strain on mother, baby, and father.

The subject of the working mother is difficult to speak or write about, especially for working fathers. One day my wife, Martha, and I were guests on a television program where we were discussing current social trends and their effect on parenting. I was asked the dreaded question, "Dr. Sears, could you comment on the working mother?" While I was trying to conjure up an answer, Martha interjected, "If I hadn't worked while you were a medical intern, you wouldn't be here now to answer that question." Women have a way of getting right to the point when addressing social issues that affect themselves and their families. My mother worked outside the home even when I was a tiny infant. As a single parent, she had to. While I strongly believe that the ideal is a full-time at-home mother, we do not live in an ideal society and the ideal is not achievable in all families. It has not been achievable in my family.

A fact of working life is that it is impossible to give one hundred percent of yourself to being a parent, a mate, and a worker. That adds up to three hundred percent. Fathers can't do it, and there's no reason mothers should be expected to. Fathers realize full well that they are constantly compromising their performance in one role in order to serve another. If mother also works outside the home, she, too, has to juggle her roles. Question: What happens if you have two jugglers as parents in the family? Answer: Baby becomes a little juggler who is required to bounce his cues and affections back and forth between various caregivers. His needs may not be consistently and predictably met and his developing sense of trust may be compromised.

JUGGLING ACT

When mother and baby are separated, both of them miss out on the full benefits of a continuous mother-infant attachment. When mother and baby spend most of their time with each other, responding positively to each other's cues, they get in harmony with each other. Each one learns to hold on to the other's attention and feel competent at communicating with one another. Not only does the mother help the baby develop, but the baby also helps the mother develop. Touching and suckling the baby cause the mother's body to produce prolactin, which may provide some biological basis for the the idea of mother's intuition. It is the frequency of suckling that raises prolactin levels, not the intensity. Scheduled "quality" time does not fulfill the biological requirements of mothering. "Quantity" time does.

There are some experts who claim that children who attend day care turn out as well as children whose mothers stay home with them all day. There are other experts who believe that home-reared children develop better (White 1985). Beware of the studies that minimize the effect of the full-time mother. The researchers are often measuring performance of certain skilled tasks, not feelings and personality development. It is difficult to measure a child's sensitivity or feelings of security and trust.

It is an amazing paradox that at the very time when researchers are becoming more aware of the value of mother-infant attachment, more mothers are returning to the work force when their children are very young. What kind of social values does this reflect? Television commercials exhort viewers to "Be all that you can be" or tell them that "You can have it all." Women (and men) are bombarded with messages that suggest that fulfillment comes from being more than "just a mother."

Many fathers I have interviewed say that they are competing with the marketplace for their wives' attention, both as a mate and as a mother of their children. The fact is that for many women the marketplace has become more attractive than the home. Today's full-time mother is often isolated in her home. She may be the only person in her building or on her block who is home all day. She and her husband may live far away from their families. Traditional societies offered mothers more support; they were surrounded by extended family members and other mothers and children who could be counted on for friendship and assistance. Adults today learn to depend on bustling offices and the companionship of co-workers to fill their needs for social interaction.

Depending on your point of view, some of these changes in today's society have been for the better and some for the worse. For the better, three times more women breastfeed today than did twenty years ago, and they breastfeed longer. They are more open about sleeping with their babies and are more likely to "wear" their babies in carriers than wheel them about in buggies. The greater emphasis on meeting baby's needs and developing an attachment style of mothering has certainly been beneficial to mother, baby, and father.

For the worse (in my opinion), more mothers are leaving home for the marketplace—either by choice or necessity. This is difficult to understand. At the very time when it seems that more and more mothers are realizing the mutual benefits of attachment parenting, more women are leaving their children in day care and working outside the home.

For the better, these changes in mothers have forced fathers to change. Women today demand more of their husbands, both as mates and as fathers for their children. I think that fathers' increased involvement benefits the family, but these role changes have confused many men, which may contribute to a divorce rate that is at an all-time high.

For the better, today's children, boys and girls, have more freedom in their choices of intellectual or vocational activity than ever before. For the worse, most of the teaching and guidance is provided by someone other than the parents.

What Can Fathers Do?

Provide emotional support. Most working mothers get more praise and recognition for a job well done at the office than for a job well done at home. The rewards of working outside the home include a title, a regular paycheck, recognition, and regular feedback about performance. The rewards of full-time mothering are immeasurably superior but not very tangible. You as a father must be responsible for giving your wife recognition and encouragement and reminding her that she is doing the most important job in the world, mothering a human being.

An example of what not to do is found in the situation at the beginning of the popular movie, *Kramer vs. Kramer*. Mrs. Kramer is a former career woman who quit her job to devote herself full-time to her first child. Meanwhile, her husband, an advertising executive on the fast track to success, is only marginally involved with his wife and child. When he is home, all he can talk about is his job. Mrs. Kramer feels increasingly isolated and unappreciated at home and leaves her husband and child in order to find a new identity for

herself. The rest of the movie places Mr. Kramer in the position of custodial single father and he learns about the stresses of being a mother the hard way—from experience.

Thus popular culture preaches the idea that total fulfillment for women comes from a job (or other outside interests) plus marriage, plus motherhood. It is difficult for fathers to counteract this idea with an equation that says: total fulfillment equals fulfillment as a wife and mother. Many women will argue that this equation is not truly balanced since it values the mother only in relation to someone else—she may be Bob's wife and Mary's mother, but who is *she*? Fathers can help balance the fulfillment equation at three points:

1. Encourage your wife in her outside interests, but help her find ways to include the baby in the things she does outside the home.

2. Be a better husband and thus increase your wife's happiness with her marriage.

3. Support and encourage her and provide recognition for her accomplishments as a mother.

Reduce the fear of divorce. Because of the alarmingly high divorce rate, women who are full-time mothers can feel very vulnerable. After all, there is a fifty percent chance that they could end up being a single mother with little or no financial support and no job security to fall back on. To protect themselves against this possibility, they juggle two careers, believing that they must keep their jobs as insurance against the future. Men must take some of the responsibility for this; to some extent fathers who are uninvolved at home have caused their wives to return to the workforce. In my experience more marriages fail because of a lack of commitment from the husband than fail because of the wife. It's time that men relearned the meaning and value of commitment to their families.

Balance your work and home commitments. It's an economic reality that time equals money and that more time spent at a job outside the home equals more money. But your absence makes things more stressful for your wife at home. If it's necessary for you to supplement your income, try to do so with work that won't separate you from your family.

Share child care. The fact is that many mothers *are* working at least part-time to supplement the family finances or to fill their own needs. If your wife is away from your baby, you must take up the slack in the baby's attachment relationship with his parents. One of the only benefits I can see to the trend toward mothers working outside the home is that fathers have been forced to assume greater involvement in caring for their children. If possible try to care for your child yourself when mother is away. But beware of the situation where father cares for the child while mother is working and vice versa. When will mother and father care for each other? The result can be like a home with two single parents, which is not a healthy model of marriage for a growing child.

Reference
White, Burton 1985. *The First Three Years of Life.* Prentice-Hall, New York.

CHAPTER 10

Where's Dad?

Even fathers who practice attachment fathering must occasionally be separated from their children, whether it's for the length of the workday or sometimes for several days at a time. Other fathers are involved in more lengthy separations from their children, are not strongly attached to them, and may be absent entirely from their children's daily lives. Separation between father and child presents unique problems in all types of father-child relationships.

Attachment Fathering and Separation

One of the side-effects of the attachment style of fathering is that the deeper the attachment between father and child, the deeper the feelings of loss when they are apart. It's not often acknowledged that these effects of separation can be felt by fathers and babies as well as by mothers and babies. If you have been involved and invested time in your baby you have created a feeling of rightness between you when you are together. It follows that you both may feel that things are not right when you are apart. A baby who doesn't feel right does not act right. When I hear a father boast, "My baby doesn't seem bothered when I'm away," I regard this as a sign of a poor attachment situation rather than a positive sign of the baby's independence. A baby who is capable of strong attachments is likely to protest when the objects of his attachment go away. When someone is missing, the structure of his whole world changes. Besides the anxiety that children feel, attached fathers also suffer uneasy feelings when they are away.

Depending on your baby's temperament, the protests may be mild and subtle or strong and obvious. Babies' sleep patterns often change when dad is away. Night-waking is more frequent and getting settled again more difficult during father's absences. Babies have more fussy periods and younger children may have more tantrums or angry outbursts. Because the whole structure of their world changes, babies' behavior may be less organized; there may be wide variations in sleeping and eating schedules.

Discipline problems often surface when dad's away. Toddlers and young children seem to temporarily "forget" the meaning of "no" and "stop" and older children seem to stretch the father-imposed limits when they are mother-enforced. High need or impulsive children of attached fathers are particularly prone to these separation behaviors. If possible, fathers should try to minimize time away from these special children.

Another effect of father's absences is that mom acts differently, especially in a home where attachment parenting is practiced. Baby gets a double whammy! Father is not there, and baby feels his absence. Mother, in reacting to her husband's absence, may seem "not all there," too. The baby may even change nursing patterns when dad's away. Some babies may react by nursing all day and all night; others may refuse the breast, and mother may experience a temporary decrease in milk production. In a house where father is the primary limit-setter, older children may take advantage of mom and test the consistency of her disciplinary standards.

Two-year-olds seem particularly sensitive to their father's absence. They may experience mood swings, from quiet withdrawal to impulsive belligerence. They may have trouble figuring out what's happening. A mother once shared with me her two-year-old's reaction to a trip her husband took. She and the child drove Daddy to the airport and waved bye-bye as his plane took off. She explained that Daddy would come back soon on the plane. The next day she found her two-year-old standing in the back yard, pointing at a plane in the sky, and yelling, "Daddy."

During a recent three-day trip of mine, I talked to my twelve-month-old son Matthew on the telephone several times. (I like to hear his babbling when I'm away from home.) Martha told me that when Matthew heard my voice he would turn his face toward the front door. She thought his expression reflected an anticipation of seeing me and disappointment when he didn't. The opening door must be a symbol of daddy's return to small children.

A Smooth Re-entry

Don't be disturbed if your baby gives you the cold shoulder when you return. This is only temporary. Babies feel a mixture of anger and confusion about separation and require

some time to adjust to your return. The first time I experienced this reaction I was devastated. I walked in the door after being away for several days, and I expected to be greeted with some "happy to see you" signs from our one-year-old. Instead, his attitude for the first few hours was more like "I could care less." I picked him up and walked with him, his head nestled into my neck. As I began to sing his favorite song, he perked up. I had struck a familiar note, and we were reunited. Sometimes you have to woo your baby back into trusting you.

Tips to Lessen the Effects of Father-Baby Separation

Consider taking your family with you when you travel. Babies are very portable and travel very easily. Home to a tiny baby is where mom and dad are, whether it's your house or a distant hotel room.

Incorporate your children into your work life instead of maintaining a strict separation of job and family. If possible, take older children with you sometimes to your job or on a business trip. It is valuable for your child to know about and feel part of your career. Let your child see you in situations where you are in the spotlight—giving a lecture, taking responsibility, doing things, being important. This is good for your child's image of you.

Leave a little bit of yourself behind. Try the following:

> Make a tape recording in which you talk and sing to your baby. Use phrases and songs that baby associates with you.
> Leave photographs of yourself.
> Call frequently to talk to your baby or child. Call around bedtime and tell a surprise bedtime story by phone.
> Suggest that your wife tell the children stories about you and your childhood while you're away.
> Don't forget to bring back presents.

My son Peter is an avid baseball fan. On each trip I try to find him a different baseball cap. His large collection may remind him that his father is away frequently, but I hope it also reminds him that while I am away I think of him.

Working from Home
One of the problems in my life has been achieving a balance between spending time with the children in my home and the children in my practice. I love them all. I hear so much about mothers feeling guilty when they leave their babies, but it seems to me that fathers get a double dose of this kind of guilt. I feel guilty when I'm away from my own children, and I feel guilty when I'm away from the children I'm responsible for in my practice. Being available is an important part of both being a pediatrician and a father.

Recently, while in the midst of building a new office, my lease expired on my old office. This time of transition between offices provided me with an opportunity to increase my availability to my family while not compromising my availability to my patients: I decided that, for a short time, I would move my office into our home. The idea for this rather unconventional professional set-up came during one of our family discussions in which we "take inventory" of how things are going with everyone. We often play the "If You Could Change Things" game. It's a way of finding out what our children are feeling and imagining and what changes may be needed. I asked our ten-year-old, Peter, to tell me what he would wish for if he could change anything. His response was, "Dad, I wish you could work at home."

The whole family helped to renovate a large area in our garage that became my temporary pediatric office. (My teenage patients call it "Doctor Bill's Garage and Body Shop.") Wanting to be sure that I made a lot of brownie points with my children, I let them know that I was moving my office into our home so that I could be closer to them. But I did impress upon them that this office was primarily for my work, and that while I was there I would be working, not playing.

What a revelation! I realized that traveling to my job every day may have been exhausting, but it was equally a therapeutic escape. Initially I missed the camaraderie of the office building—the mutual stroking and recognition that goes on between colleagues in elevators and hallways or during coffee or lunch breaks. Now, with my office at home, when I wasn't with my patients, my social world was just my family. Even though I could escape into my garage, I had to relate to my family all day long and I was not accustomed to this. Having my office in my home opened my eyes to another unfortunate effect of social changes in our industrial society. When fathers are forced to leave their homes for the marketplace they lose the ability to relate to their families on a day-to-day basis. They become more comfortable with the social interactions of their workplace. This experience also helped me understand why a former career woman often feels isolated when she becomes a full-time mother and stays home with a baby all day long.

It is important for your child to know where your priorities are. Even though you may need to work away from home your child should understand that your home is more important. Being absent by necessity is pardonable; being absent by choice is not. Fathering is indeed an at-home job.

Absent Fathers

The absence of a father in the home presents special problems for children. Although both boys and girls are affected, father's absence seems to have more of an effect on boys than girls. In one study, boys were found to have more difficulty in assuming masculine roles when they were separated from their fathers in early childhood. Boys seem to be particularly vulnerable to father's absence during early developmental stages when they are learning to control their own impulses. Boys between the ages of twelve and thirty months show more aggressive behavior when their fathers are absent. Researchers believe that young boys need a father at particular stages of personality development to help them control their inborn masculine aggressive tendencies. Sleep disturbances such as nightmares and fears are often common when fathers are gone. Boys experience **father hunger;**

The Change Happened Almost Overnight

My husband's testimonial is very short and to the point. "I was angry with Kandis because she cried a lot. So after I started treating her better she was happy again." He really doesn't like to talk about it. I hope you don't mind if I tell the story from my point of view:

When we moved here from San Francisco before Thanksgiving our youngest daughter Kandis took the move rather hard. It wasn't noticeable at first but she gradually became more and more cranky and cantankerous. This made Mark very irritated and he would make comments such as "Yeah, she sure isn't my favorite child" or he would call her "Crybaby." But he would never ever hold her, kiss her, or even talk to her in a positive manner. It was all negative attention. During the holidays our marriage hit a crisis point and there was much emotional upheaval going on inside myself. I nursed Kandis about twice a day at naptime and bedtime. She never asked for it any other time so I thought she was weaning herself.

After the rush of the holidays was over, Kandis became sick with the flu and then a bad chest cold. She was totally drained and looked it. Her crying had increased and she never smiled or laughed. I was worried but I thought she'd perk up after she was well. Mark would sit her on the couch and tell her to "shut up, shut up" angrily.

She was still fighting a bit of a chest cold when she fell off a counter. After taking her to the emergency room, the doctors who examined her couldn't help but notice her weakened condition. I was referred to you and you gave me many ideas as to what was going on with her and what I should do about it. I did two things specifically. Number One I fed her five to six times a day on the breast whether she wanted it or not. (My milk supply increased tremendously.) Number Two I had a nice little talk with my husband. I told him it was important to give Kandis some love and attention and to give her lots of positive talking and touching. At first he was skeptical but he agreed that something had to change. His efforts were strained at first. I could tell it wasn't easy for him. But she picked up on it right away and returned the positive attention. Believe me the change in her happened almost overnight. From whining, lethargic, and sickly to happy, bubbly, laughing, silly, and healthy. She gained almost three pounds in one month. People would say things like, "Does she do anything besides smile all day?" or "She sure is a happy kid," and "Look at her smile!" The snowball effect went the other direction. The more Kandis smiled at Daddy, the more sincere and affectionate Daddy became. Kandis sure loves her Daddy now and Daddy definitely loves her.

Mark thought he was doing the right thing by being tough. He doesn't like to admit he was wrong. But he knows; he can't help but know. It's so obvious. Your methods really do work.

---

some inner fear threatens to overwhelm them and leads to a specific longing for father (Herzog 1980).

Girls reared in homes where the father is absent show a higher incidence of difficulties in later interactions with males. Boys from homes where fathers were absent were described by their teachers as less advanced in moral development (Lamb 1981). Studies have also shown that mothers without husbands assert more power over their children, probably because they must. They are required to be the "heavy" in discipline disputes. Children of absent fathers tend to respond less to mothers' disciplinary measures. Having a father around who will back up mothers' decisions gives her credibility and increases the likelihood that the child will respect her discipline.

Fathers have their own unique contribution to make to infant development as do infants to their fathers' development. When father is absent, neither baby nor father develops as well.

References:

Herzog, J. Sleep disturbances and father hunger in 18-28-month-old boys. *Psychoanalytic Study of the Child*, Vol 35, 219-33, 1980
Lamb, M.E., Editor *The Role of the Father in Child Development*. John Wiley: New York, 1981.

CHAPTER 11

Father's Role in Discipline

Fathers play a vital role in discipline by providing balance and structure in the otherwise disorganized world of the child.

Discipline is one of the most confused concepts in child-rearing. Fathers often feel that discipline is something restrictive you do to a child—a punishment or some kind of external force that will keep the child in line. "Spare the rod and spoil the child"—how often fathers have heard these words. Too much emphasis has been placed on punishment from the rod, especially in the heavy-handed advice often given to fathers. While "rod therapy" may be a small part of discipline for some families, in this book I hope to guide fathers into a style of discipline that lessens the need for punishment and maximizes the father's positive influence. Behind a heavy hand there must be a warm heart.

I feel that discipline should encompass more positive impulses such as teaching, direction, guidance, feeling right, and

trust. Your goal in disciplining your child is to create an attitude within your child and an atmosphere in your home such
that punishment is seldom necessary. Still, as adults know,
punishment will sometimes be necessary as children grow
and learn. But if a father follows the positive principles of
effective discipline, the punishment will be administered
wisely and appropriately.

Fathers must change their attitude toward discipline. Consider first how to help your child learn self-discipline and willing obedience and then decide how to redirect or discipline
your child if disobedience and defiance occur.

Discipline Begins at Birth

Larry, a first-time father, brought his one-year-old baby in for
a checkup. After examining the baby, I asked Larry if he had
any concerns or questions. He had one: "When should we
begin discipline? The baby's into everything." My response
was, "You have been disciplining your child since the moment of birth."

I recently presented a four-part educational seminar for
new parents. Although the seminar was titled "How to Discipline Your Child," during the first three evenings I spoke
mainly about the topics covered in earlier chapters of this
book: responding promptly to a baby's cry, breastfeeding
and not weaning before the child is ready, sleeping with your
baby, "wearing" your baby in a baby carrier—the whole attachment style of parenting. I deliberately avoided mention-
ing the word discipline until near the end of the course. In
the last session of the seminar, I overheard a father complaining, "When are we going to get on to talking about discipline so I can learn to handle my unruly kid!" I had actually
been talking all along about building strong discipline on
the cornerstone of knowing your child and helping your child
feel right. I had been trying to help them see that effective
discipline begins at birth.

"I want to be the authority figure in our home," replied
a new father in response to my question about what fathers

wanted to learn most about discipline. Authority is based upon trust. In order for your child to regard you as an authority figure he must first trust you. This is where your style of parenting during the first year really pays off. Babies who know that distress is consistently followed by comfort, that cries are heard and responded to, that needs are filled unconditionally, and that their own disorganization is brought to order by nurturing and responsive caregivers learn to trust their caregiving environment. Trust leads to the development of an inner feeling of rightness that forms the basis of baby's behavior. A baby who feels right on the inside is more likely to act right on the outside. A child's outward behavior mirrors his inner feelings.

One day while examining a one-year-old, I noticed the mutual trust that was apparent in how the parents, Jan and David, related to their child. They had been practicing the attachment style of parenting since birth, and David was a very involved and committed father. I was unable to contain my admiration for this family and exclaimed, "You're good disciplinarians." Surprised, David responded, "But we don't spank our child!" I had to explain that I was using the term disciplinarian in a positive sense to describe the trust that had developed between parents and child.

The attachment style of parenting helps mothers and fathers to know their children better. By being available and responsive to your baby during the first year you learn to read your baby's cues. You learn to anticipate the behavior that will follow certain cues from the baby. You learn to interpret what your baby is feeling by watching how he is acting. Learning to read the feelings behind a baby's actions sets the stage for a very important part of discipline in the older child: determining the feelings behind a child's actions.

What happens to the baby whose cues are not consistently nor appropriately responded to? The baby whose distress is not followed by comfort and who cannot count on a predictable response from his caregivers? This baby operates from a basis of mistrust instead of trust, anxiety rather than rightness. The end result of this kind of parenting, based on restrained responses to a baby's needs, is an angry baby. The most difficult children to discipline are those who operate from a basis of anger formed during their early years. Angry children breed parents who are also prone to anger when they discipline.

The more restrained style of parenting not only produces a child who does not feel right; it also causes parents not to know their child as well. When they do not permit themselves to respond intuitively to their baby, they fail to learn to read their child's behavior during the first year and are less likely to be able to understand him later on.

"But won't we spoil our baby if we hold him a lot and pick him up every time he cries?" asked a worried father. The fear of spoiling has put a damper on the natural art of parenting. Spoiling is a word that should be forever stricken from parenting books. It describes something put on a shelf and left to rot. Babies do not get spoiled by being held. Babies spoil if they are not held. The attachment style of parenting is more likely to produce a socially and emotionally stable child who is easier to discipline.

What about Obedience?

Some fathers feel that it is (or should be) the nature of a child to obey. A child must obey simply because he is a child. While you may wish that this was true, it isn't. Real obedience is motivated by respect. Respect is based on trust and the foundation of trust is laid during the first year of life. Obedience without respect does not lead to healthy discipline. You can beat a child into obedience, but you cannot force a child to respect his father.

Respect for authority is a hallmark of effective discipline. Respect means to feel or show esteem for, to honor. The attachment style of parenting during the first year of life leads the child to honor or respect his parents. Fathers may not think they are disciplining when they pick up a crying baby, but they are. The tiny baby whose distress signals are listened to learns that his caregivers are in charge of helping and organizing him. A child must know who's in charge. The parents who show that they are in charge of a crying baby by attending to his needs are more likely to be the ones who take charge of a distressed child as well. Caring for your baby during the first year of life truly prepares a father for the many disciplinary encounters in later years. Learning how to sensitively console the colicky baby prepares you for taking charge of the toddler during a temper tantrum. Dads, get hooked on your babies! Carrying your baby, consoling your baby, playing with your baby, loving your baby—that's discipline!

"Announcing Mr. and Mrs. Van Gleasen . . . and . . . Master Van Gleason."

Taking baby with you when he's small builds a foundation for discipline in the years ahead.

Disciplining Your Toddler

If you have developed a sensitivity to your baby during the first year of life and gotten to know him and helped him feel right, disciplining him as a toddler is much easier. During the first year the roles of mother and father are primarily those of caregivers and nurturers. During the second year, toddlerhood, father's role widens into that of an authority figure and a designer of your child's environment.

Realistic Expectations of Toddler Behavior

Fathers are often confused about what toddlers are really like. They often confuse normal toddler curiosity with misbehavior. Fathers' unrealistic expectations of toddler behavior often lead to mother-father conflicts. Mothers usually are more accepting of a wide range of normal toddler behavior whereas fathers tend to place more restrictions on young children. This is not always bad. A more restrictive father helps to balance an overly tolerant mother.

Toddlers are driven by intense curiosity which overrules consideration of safety. One of father's roles in discipline is to protect the toddler from his own impulses. Toddlers are naturally impulsive. That's how they learn.

"Why won't he mind me?" shouted John, frustrated with his one-year-old who was crawling up and pulling the papers

off the top of the desk. "No, no, no," shouted Mike for the tenth time as his exploring one-and-a-half-year-old lurched towards the television knobs. These normal hassles occur every day between father and child. Here are some tips that will protect your child from his environment and the environment from your child.

How to Say "No"
Sometime between twelve and fifteen months, most babies can understand that "no" means they should stop doing what they're doing. The "en" sound seems to be a universal expression of displeasure. I have heard eight-month-old babies exclaim "Na-na-na" to protest having their faces washed or their diapers changed.

Toddlers can usually understand that "no" means not to do what they're doing, but they seldom understand the reason why they should not pull off the television knobs or tug on the lamp cord. Developing mutual sensitivity between father and infant during the first year really pays off when it is time to discipline the toddler in order to protect him from his environment. While infants less than a year and a half do not say many intelligible words (the term infant is derived from a Latin word meaning "non-speaking one"), most toddlers do understand your body language and tone of voice. If your baby has grown accustomed to your usual tone of voice during play, he will be uniquely sensitive to your language of displeasure. You don't have to yell "No" in an angry, harsh, and upsetting tone of voice. If you have developed this mutual sensitivity, a firm "No, stop, don't touch" accompanied by picking the baby up, looking him squarely in the eye, and removing him from the scene of the crime will usually get the point across.

Fathers, keep in mind that some babies take longer to get the point than others. You may have to perform the say-no-and-remove-him sequence ten times before it actually sinks in. (It might be easier to move the television set and other temptations to a higher place until your child is older.) When his relentless pursuit of the dangling light cord has been thwarted, your toddler may throw a tantrum in protest, but don't let this shake you. If you have built up a trusting relationship during the first year, it will not be threatened by a few tantrums. Fathers are often confused as to how much of their discipline really gets through to toddlers. A rule of thumb is to imagine how much of your message you think gets through and then double it. Toddlers understand far more than we think they do. In most babies, receptive language development (the ability to understand what is spoken) is six months ahead of expressive language (the ability to speak). In disciplining your curious toddler, you'll have to balance the right amount of freedom to explore his environment with the restraints necessary to prevent him from hurting himself or his environment. Toddlers need and expect this protection from both mother and father.

Handling Temper Tantrums

Why do young children throw tantrums? Tantrum-like behavior results when a child encounters a conflict between what he wants to do and what he is capable of doing. The toddler wants to walk and explore and get his hands on everything in the environment, but the intense desire to explore often exceeds his capabilities. This leads to frustration. Being able to get around by himself makes the toddler feel big and grown-up. This propels him to test the limits of his environment: to turn knobs, pull on tablecloths, climb up on tables. The toddler does not think first of right and wrong or the safety of his actions. He is simply driven to act. When someone descends on him suddenly (someone he loves and trusts) with a loud "No," a conflict of wills results.

The strong-willed toddler seldom respects a second opinion from you. Although he wants to feel big and powerful, his environment tells him how small he really is. He does not yet have the ability to express his anger in language, so he does so through action—a tantrum. The outward show of emotions such as anger and frustration is a newly found ability which your toddler should be free to express and learn from.

A child is off-balance during a tantrum and needs a parent to help him regain his control. He is screaming and flailing his arms, and his behavior disintegrates right in front of you. Shocked parents often feel helpless to stop the process. The body language of a child during a tantrum seems to say, "Help me, I'm out-of-control. Protect me from myself." Meanwhile frustrated parents are asking, "How?" Sometimes you won't be able to handle your child's tantrums, and he must learn for himself how to regain control. Dad can simply be available for support when the emotionally drained child needs refueling. More often, when your child is screaming and out of control he needs someone stronger to take charge. Pick your child up, hold him firmly and lovingly while you talk to him in a controlled voice. Give him a caring message such as, "Johnny, you're upset, Daddy wants to help, and I'm going to hold you until you stop crying, because I love you." Your child may initially kick and protest your taking charge but then will realize that you're in control and will finally melt exhausted in your arms. This will reinforce your child's feelings of trust in you. Taking charge of a two-year-old's tantrum is similar to comforting the colicky infant. You show your child that you are powerful but non-threatening by giving your child the message that you care and therefore you are going to take charge. This is the same message that fathers should convey to their children even as newborns: distress is followed by comfort.

Above all avoid a shouting match. Your child is already out of control and needs someone older and wiser to stay on top of things. Staying calm may be especially difficult for fathers since tantrums pose a threat to their authority and power. ("How can this tiny child turn me into an emotional wreck?") Being unable to stop a child's tantrum can lead to outbursts of anger from a father. I have seen occasions where the child throws a tantrum, father responds by starting a shouting match, pretty soon both are out of control, and mother has to take charge of both "children." This scene is not healthy role-modeling for the observant child. Temper tantrums usually subside around two to three years of age when your child becomes more verbal and is able to express his feelings with words rather than actions.

Father's Role in Setting Limits

A very important role for fathers in discipline is to lay down a strong foundation by nurturing their babies and then use this foundation to set limits for the developing child. Every facet of discipline is built on the nurturing relationship between the father and child in the first two years of life. Nurture combined with limit-setting creates feelings of fairness and security within the child. The child is, by nature, impulsive; nurture without limit-setting leaves a child to flounder in a sea of uncertainty, having no direction, no goals, and little fulfillment. For a child, there is security in limits.

Limit-setting without nurture also fails. If a father comes across only as a "no" person, heavy-handed, stern, punitive, and authoritarian, his discipline will have little lasting effect. In the numerous studies that have looked at the effects of fathers' early input on child outcome, the appropriate dosages of nurture (also known as affection) and limit-setting stand out as important contributors to the emotional and social well-being of the child. Sometimes fathers are hesitant to become too affectionate and nurturing for fear that the child will become manipulative and will never learn to obey. Actually, the opposite is true. *Being affectionate allows fathers to be more firm about setting limits.* Early involvement and nurturing make the trust between father and child so strong that setting appropriate limits is easier for dads to do and children to accept.

LIMIT SETTING + NURTURING = EFFECTIVE DISCIPLINE

LIMIT SETTING − NURTURING = INEFFECTIVE DISCIPLINE

In the usual confused, chaotic, and disorganized world of the child, father provides structure and discipline. A child wants and needs limits set by a trusted person in authority. Picture what is going on in this young bundle of energy, driven in all directions by whim and impulse. If a child's energy is not harnessed he will waste it by going in many frivolous directions, often exerting a lot of effort but achieving little. However, if there is structure in his life the child feels more secure because someone has channeled his energies in a meaningful direction.

Explaining the rules.   Take the case of Erin, a three-year-old who has been known to ride her tricycle out into the street. How should a father handle this problem? First, it is important that children have a clear understanding of what is expected of them and, if possible, why. Before the child is allowed to ride the tricycle father performs two acts of discipline:

1. Provide the child with clearly defined limits as to when and where she may ride her tricycle and what the consequences are if she disobeys.

2. Be sure the child understands your directions by having her repeat them. Often children are not willfully defiant but rather show childish irresponsibility by "forgetting."

Dad's instructions might go something like this: "Erin, because Mommy and Daddy love you very much, we don't want you to get squashed by a car. You must ride your tricycle only in these places. [Notice that I used the positive direction—where she should ride—and not a negative direction—where she should not.] Because we love you, I want you to promise me that you will only ride your tricycle in these places. Do you understand, Erin?"

Meanwhile, you are holding your child and looking her squarely in the eye with the firm voice of authority and a caring look of affection. Wait for her response and be sure that she clearly repeats your directions. She has been given a framework to operate in that she understands. As a trusted authority figure you then add, "I don't expect to see you riding your tricycle in the street. That would make Dad very unhappy, and I would put the tricycle in the garage for a long time and you couldn't ride it." It is vitally important that the child understand the nature of what you expect of him or her and the consequences of disobedience.

The older child. A helpful way to explain rules to an older child is to use the analogy of playing a game they are familiar with. The conversation with your child might go something like this.

"Mary, any time a group of people live and play together, they must have rules. Otherwise people get hurt and nobody has any fun.

"It's like your soccer game. You have to play by the rules or you get penalized. If you step out of bounds you lose the ball. If you trip some other child on purpose you are penalized because you have violated her rights. The coaches and the referees make the rules and all of you players agree to play by these rules before the game starts."

Mary gives you the understanding nod you expect, even though she wonders what you are getting at. It's important during any disciplinary conversation to check that your child understands what you are trying to say.

"This is the way our home is going to operate, Mary. Everybody in our home has rights, and we all need to respect each other's rights. Mom and Dad are going to make the rules, and as long as you are a member of the family you must abide by these rules. Just as in the soccer game, if you don't stick to the rules there are penalties. [You then describe what the rules are, along with the corresponding penalties.]

"As you get older the rules may change, just as the boundaries on your soccer field get longer and wider as you get bigger. But you must still stay in bounds."

The family council. What can you do when the family is all out of harmony with each other and discipline has gotten out of hand? Call together the whole family for a family council. After dinner is a good time. Set the stage for your concerns by stating, "Dad has noticed some problems lately. We're going to straighten these out tonight. . . ." First, ask each child if he or she has any points they would like to discuss. (Let them feel free to voice their concerns, too.) Address their concerns then relate your concerns and mom voices hers. End the family council by stating what behaviors need to change, exactly what you expect, and the consequence if you don't see improvement. This is not a scolding session. It is simply necessary that when many people live close together, some social rules are in order. Most large families need family councils at least every other month.

Defining Expected Behavior

Although I feel that fathers should play the major role in discipline, in most families it is mothers who are with the children more and who therefore carry out most discipline because they are more available.

Take the example of the frazzled mother and the defiant child. Father comes home at the end of the day and is greeted by a mother who is worn out from the incessant "I won'ts" of a defiant child. Before he leaves for work the next day father conveys to the child caringly but with a voice of authority the following points:

1. What behavior he expects.

2. The consequences if the child doesn't behave this way.

3. The rewards if he does.

4. A message of support for mom, such as, "I love your Mommy very much, and I will not tolerate your talking back to her."

I believe that discipline in the family should be structured in such a way that fathers lay down the directions. Even when mother carries out the limit-setting, the child should feel that the original orders came from father. This gets mother off the hook. In many households discipline is entirely up to the mother because she is with the children so much and father is around so little. Mother often takes the role of the bad guy and father's role is all fun and games. This is not effective role-modeling for children, nor is it healthy discipline. The child becomes confused and then learns to play one parent against the other while respecting neither.

Fathers can get mothers out of the bad-guy trap. When you set the limits for your child's behavior, you take pressure off mother and allow her to be more effective in her primary roles as nurturer and designer of the child's environment and her secondary role as discipline administrator. Beware of the situation where father "performs" discipline ceremonies when mother is there as a witness but becomes a real pushover when he is alone with the child. Limit-setting is most effective when clear directions are given to the child both in the mother's presence and in private times between father and child. Mother feels better knowing that father has clearly defined the behavior expected of the child and the child feels more secure not getting mixed messages.

Many studies support the fact that consistent and fair limits set by father increase the chances of a child developing a healthy level of self-esteem. One study found that the development of leadership, responsibility, and social maturity in adolescent males is closely associated with a father-son relationship that is not only nurturing but also includes a strong component of limit-setting (Bronfenbrenner 1961). In another study the adolescent boys who scored high in masculine interest were more likely to say that their fathers set limits for them than boys who scored low (Lamb 1981).

Staying on course. Using analogies that relate to your child's special interests can help you illustrate why children need discipline. Here's a space story that I have used with my ten-year-old son, Peter.

A father needs a nurturing relationship with his child in order to establish effective discipline.

"Peter, I love you very much. You will never completely realize how much a father loves his children until you have children of your own. Because I love you, there are certain goals that I want you to achieve, and one of these goals is that you will obey Mom and Dad. This will help you some-day reach your goal of being in charge of yourself, knowing what is right and wrong, and making right decisions.

"The way I discipline you is very much like the way the spaceship, Apollo, reached the moon. The main reason that Apollo was able to reach its goal was that there were a lot of people at the space center in Houston, constantly monitor-ing the path of that spaceship. If the spaceship strayed off the path a bit, there was someone there, like a father, to guide the spaceship back on course. If there hadn't been anyone to guide the ship, it would still be going around in circles, traveling in Never-Never Land.

"Dad is going to be like one of those spaceship moni-tors. If I see you straying off course, I'm going to step in and help you get back on the course. If I don't, you're not going to reach your goals, you're not going to be very happy as a child, and I wouldn't be a very good father. Because I care about you very much, I'm going to stick by you to help you reach your goals. When you can set your own course, you won't need Dad to monitor you anymore. But even then it will be nice to know that you have a back-up system on the ground—your dad—in case your own controls fail."

As your children grow, continue teaching them to con-trol their impulses. Today's children grow up in a "gimme" world of material overindulgence and instant gratification. Failure to control impulses gets most children (and adults) into trouble. The best way to teach your child to control his impulses is to model this behavior yourself. This is not al-ways easy for fathers to do.

There's a lot of wisdom in the old saying that the only difference between men and boys is the price of their toys. My weakness is boats—big boats! Sailing has always been our family hobby, and after our move to California I wanted to buy a large sailboat. I went through all kinds of mental gymnastics in order to justify the purchase by proving that our family needed (or *I* needed) a very large sailboat. Ultimately I decided to purchase a smaller boat that was more manageable financially. (The wisdom of my wife prevailed.) Soon after, I asked our son Bob, then twelve years old, if he was disappointed that I had not bought the big boat. Since Bob was going through the impulsive preadolescent stage, I expected him to voice his disappointment that we hadn't gone all out and bought the big boat. To my amazement and delight, Bob responded, "Yes, Dad, I sure liked that big sailboat, but we didn't need it. The smaller one is good enough, and we can use the money in better ways." I was glad I had not given way to my own impulses and thus set up an unhealthy role model for my son. Dads are always on stage in front of their children.

Corrective Discipline

If you devote your time and energy to laying a foundation of trust and sensitivity within your child in the early years of life, corrective discipline will be less necessary. If you have been a nurturing father who has supported your child through infancy and two-year-old tantrums and have set limits, provided structure, and reinforced desirable behavior, your child will have become accustomed to an inner feeling of rightness. He will act in the right way because acting right reinforces this feeling. The child is internally motivated to behave in a desirable way.

However, there will be times that your child will stray into undesirable behavior, and you will find yourself needing to apply corrective discipline. At this point you may be thinking that I am finally going to get down to discussing spanking. Not yet! I want to talk about another kind of corrective discipline called chastening.

Chastening Versus Punishing

There is a difference between chastening and punishing. Any disciplinary action has three goals:

1. To stop undesirable behavior.

2. To promote the desired behavior.

3. To leave a child feeling right with himself and with the disciplinarian.

Punishment alone accomplishes only one of these goals: it stops undesirable behavior, at least for the moment. Punishment is a penalty for an offense of the rules. It may or may not focus on redirecting the child's future behavior. Punishment may not always leave the child feeling right, especially when it is carried out in anger without regard for the child's feelings.

Chastening attempts to achieve all three goals. It means getting inside your child, figuring out why he is misbehaving, and redirecting him toward more desirable behavior. You chasten your child out of love and concern; chastening leaves the child feeling right and trusting the authority figures in his life. It gives your child this message: "I'm your father and one of my many jobs is to see that you obey. Because I love you and care about you, I want you to act right and I'm going to help you obey." In order to chasten your child, you have to find out what's going on inside of him, what prompted his action, and how he feels as a result of what he did. Chastening redirects the child along the path you want him to go; punishment penalizes him for taking the wrong path.

Let me illustrate the difference between punishment and chastening by describing an incident which occurred in my own family. One Christmas morning when our daughter Hayden was five years old, she was excitedly prancing around, jingling a set of sleigh bells. Suddenly, eight-year-old Peter's forehead got in the way of those bells, and he let out a howl of indignation. Peter assumed that Hayden had hit him on the head intentionally, and he protested loudly to us and to Hayden.

From the looks on our faces, Hayden was vaguely aware she had done something wrong, but she felt certain that she hadn't meant to. Martha, my wife, told Hayden to stop swinging the bells around and see if her brother was hurt. She immediately stiffened and resisted her mother's command as Martha explained that the way she was playing with the bells was not safe and requested that Hayden tell Peter she was sorry. Hayden shook her head "no" and got an insulted look on her face. Martha said, "You must still say you are sorry even if you didn't mean to hurt Peter, and you need to ask him if he is all right. You must care if he is hurting."

Our looks and Peter's howling must have made Hayden feel that she had been unjustly accused, because she continued to refuse to apologize. We told her that she wouldn't be able to open her presents until she had made things right with her brother. At this point, Martha and I were in agreement that Hayden had not meant to hurt Peter but that she still should say she was sorry for hurting him accidentally. But by this time the situation had become a conflict of wills. Hayden's pride was on the line, and she grew more and more resistant to apologizing. Our authority was also at stake because we had previously been consistent about expecting and demanding apologies; we insist that our children demonstrate an "I care" attitude when they hurt another child, whether by accident or intentionally. They also know that defiance of reasonable authority is not tolerated in our home. As parents who believe in immediate disciplinary action, especially for defiance, we were caught in a dilemma: should we punish or chasten Hayden in this situation?

At this point, no matter how hard I tried, my anger was getting the better of my wisdom. I was not going to let this defiant little kid ruin our Christmas morning. I considered taking Hayden into our bedroom and spanking her then and there. But neither my wife nor I felt right about this approach. Martha said to me, "I know Hayden well, and something inside her is not right. For one thing she usually does not have any trouble apologizing or forgiving." I agreed.

By now, Hayden had become hysterical and was thumping her fists on the floor and crying out "No, no, no!" This made Martha and me certain that spanking was not the correct approach. Our anger at her defiance subsided, and we realized we had a frightened little girl on our hands who had completely lost control of her actions. There was more at stake than her pride.

What helped me most at this point was focusing not on my own anger at not being able to control my daughter, but focusing instead on my daughter's feelings. I realized that I had to take charge of Hayden because she could not take charge of herself. I held her tightly in my arms to control her kicking and flailing and explained very calmly but firmly that she was going to have to ask her brother's forgiveness or she would have to sit on the couch and watch while everyone else opened their presents. My firm but caring hold on her, my gentle tone of voice, and direct eye contact conveyed a dual message: "I care and I'm in charge here, but I'm going to stick by you until we all feel right about this situation." She calmed down somewhat, but she still refused to comply with our request to apologize to her brother.

Meanwhile my wife was analyzing Hayden as only an intuitive mother can. Martha looked her straight in the eyes and I put my hand on her shoulder as we both surrounded her with structure and security—as if to protect her from herself. We explained to her that we understood how hard it is sometimes to say you're sorry. Martha told Hayden a story, "When I was a little girl, I refused to apologize to my sister, but my parents didn't know how to help me, so I just stayed miserable all day in my pride and anger."

As we spoke to her in voices of caring authority, Hayden calmed down and listened. Soon she muttered a tiny "sorry" to her brother. I encouraged her to expand on this apology by looking at him, touching his hand, and saying, "I'm sorry, Peter, if I hurt you, even though I didn't mean to." Peter replied, "That's all right." He accepted the apology as he knew we expected him to do. (This restores the feeling of rightness and justice in the one who has apologized.) We all held each other, affirming our love for Hayden and being thankful that the battle was over.

Early in this incident, our other children were observing the conflict with the usual childish snickers: "Boy, is Hayden gonna get it." They knew that defiance was not tolerated in our household. But as they saw us getting to the root of the problem and their sister beginning to feel better, they became more interested in helping Hayden feel right than in witnessing her punishment. The sensitive attitude of our older children eased Hayden's embarrassment as we all came together and held hands as a family. At the end of this drama there was a feeling of rightness that prevailed through the entire family.

This chastening took about half an hour. I could have handled the whole ordeal with a spanking which would have taken only a few minutes. If I had spanked Hayden for her defiance, I would have accomplished only one thing: the next time, perhaps, she may not have been so defiant. She might still have refused to apologize after the spanking, and then what would I have done? Spank her harder until she apologized out of fear? This would have left the whole family feeling out of sorts. We would have had an angry, embarrassed little girl with a sore bottom and an angry father with a sore hand. The older children would have witnessed a superficial and ineffective method of discipline, but one they would likely carry into their own parenting experiences. All in all, it would have been a lousy way to start Christmas Day.

What did Hayden learn from the chastening? She learned that defiance would not go undisciplined. More importantly, she learned that her father would take control when she couldn't. Most important of all, she learned that her father cared enough to understand her feelings and redirect them toward rightness. What did I learn? First, I learned that my anger could make me act impulsively and want to settle discipline problems with a quick spanking. I also learned that my pride could overcome my wisdom if I let it. (I wasn't going to let this little kid say no to her big and powerful father.) The main thing I learned from this dramatic Christmas morning was the importance of investing time and energy during critical moments such as these, when modeling a firm but caring style of paternal authority will have a lasting effect on the whole family. Punishment is an action. Chastening is an investment.

References

Bronfenbrenner, U. Some familial antecedents of responsibility and leadership in adolescents. In Petrullos, L. and Bass, B. M., eds., *Leadership and Interpersonal Behavior*. New York: Holt, Rinehart, and Winston, 1961.

Lamb, M. E., ed. *The Role of the Father in Child Development*. New York: Wiley, 1981.

CHAPTER 12

Father as a Role Model

A model is an example to be imitated. Children imitate models whether they are good or bad. Being a good role model means providing your child with an example of behavior that is genuine, consistent, and worth copying.

Fathers are always on stage performing in front of their children. Fathers who have developed a strong trusting relationship with their children beginning in infancy are the ones most likely to be influential role models. A person does not try to imitate someone he or she does not trust. Once you have committed yourself to the attachment style of fathering, your child is hooked on you and you have to live up to your end of the commitment.

A father who is less involved does not develop a strong trusting relationship with his child. Therefore, he is less influential as a role model. This may explain why some children paradoxically do not appear to be highly affected by weak paternal role models.

Father as Nurturer

In surveying the many studies of paternal role modeling, one fact stands out: The role of the father as nurturer is the foundation of all the other ways in which a father serves as a role model. The father will be a more effective model as a male, as a disciplinarian, as a decision-maker, and as a family leader if he has been and continues to be nurturing and affectionate with his child from infancy on. Again, this is because early nurturing builds trust, and trust forms the basis of all subsequent relationships.

Have you hugged your child today? The essentials of the nurturing style of fathering are touching, eye contact, and focused attention. There seems to be a general tendency to touch children less as they grow older. We should naturally go from holding our children in infancy to hugging them during childhood and adolescence. If you really want to get a point across to your child, put your hand on his shoulder and look him straight in the eye when you talk with him. Address your child by name; this gives him a feeling of importance.

From your example, your child will learn to touch people with his eyes, hands, and heart. No matter what occupation your child goes into, the ability to connect with people is a valuable asset. A father's failure to model this nurturing style may lead to a child being detached and "wimpy" in interpersonal relationships.

In interviews, children often describe fathers as punitive and restricting while mothers are described as sensitive and understanding. This narrow view of fathers is unfair but, perhaps, deserved. By taking a more nurturing role in child care, fathers can indeed improve their children's image of the paternal role, an image which is likely to carry over into how their grandchildren are fathered.

Father as Comforter

The importance of modeling tenderness for children, especially boys, was shown to us one day in a heartwarming situation involving our son, Jim, who was sixteen years old at the time. Martha and I were in the kitchen when we heard nine-month-old Erin crying in our bedroom. Since we believe that crying should be promptly ministered to, Martha and I headed quickly toward the bedroom. Upon arriving at the bedroom door we saw a beautiful sight: there was Jim, our almost-grown athlete, lying down next to Erin, stroking her head and consoling her as she stopped crying. Why was Jim comforting Erin? Because he had seen from our behavior that when babies cry, adults listen and respond.

Mothers usually rate top billing as the family comforter. How common it is to see an injured two-year-old bypass dad

Dads need to model comforting behavior in order to model strength.

and run straight for mom. This is to be expected since this pattern of care has been imprinted on the child from birth. When babies cry they are immediately offered that greatest of pacifiers, the breast. It is hard for a dad to match that. Because dads feel inadequate as comforters early in infancy, we often fall into the pattern of letting mom always be the comforter, and the child learns that he should head for mother when he is upset. Even if dads attempt to function as comforters in early infancy, babies still will initially prefer mom, but at least they will learn that mom is not the only comforter in the house. Comforter comes from a Latin word that means "to give strength." If dads are to be models of strength they also need to model comfort. This is especially important for sons. A boy needs to grow up learning to be sensitive. He needs to balance assertiveness with tenderness. Daughters also relate to these qualities in a father, and they are likely to seek out this balance in their own mates.

Father as Decision-Maker

Provide a model of decisiveness for your child. The growing child should see that important family matters require a mutual decision-making process that involves both mom and dad, but I believe that dad is primarily responsible for making decisions. A passive father is an ineffective role model for his children. When it comes to privileges and limit-setting, children can be very crafty about playing one parent against the other. ("But Mom said I could!") Children are less confused when parents agree ahead of time and act together. This makes it easier for them to trust their parents to be in charge.

Father as a Model of Emotional Expression

Children are especially susceptible to the emotion of anger. While occasional and quickly resolved anger is a normal healthy emotion, persistent and unresolved anger is not. When I counsel families where parents complain that "my child is always angry," usually I can trace the roots of the children's behavior to unresolved anger in one or both of the parents. An impulsive father told me that having children had forced him to learn to control his own outbursts of anger.

In Times of Crisis

Our family hobby is sailing. One summer we took a family cruise along the east coast of the United States from Maine to South Carolina. As we enjoyed a leisurely sail down the East River in New York, we sailed past the Statue of Liberty and I sat with my two older sons on the bow of the boat, relating the history behind the statue and how fortunate we were to live in such a great country as the United States. As darkness began to fall the thrill of sailing within a hundred yards of the Statue of Liberty soon turned into an entirely different situation, one that sailors dread: fog. As we sailed from the mouth of the East River out into the ocean we were enveloped in a pea-soup fog which limited our visiblity to around twenty or thirty feet. We were sailing through one of the busiest shipping channels in the world, but I wasn't worried about a collision with another boat because we had a very effective radar system. A few hours later, however, the radar stopped working. Modern technology had failed us, leaving us vulnerable to a collision with another boat.

A father is allowed to be scared, but not out of control. I was scared, but I tried to keep my panic under control as I summoned my two sons to help me work on the radar. As we worked furiously and prayed even more furiously, the radar screen came back on, and we proceeded safely through the fog. My sons could see the sweat on my face and the fear in my eyes, but I tried to balance these normal reactions with the secure sense that I was in charge. In crisis situations, fear transfers easily from father to child because the child looks to the father as the gauge of the situation. Similarly, the father's sense of being in control will also extend to the child and help to calm fear.

Modeling Priorities for Your Children

I deeply regret that in the early days of my fathering and medical careers, I put my profession first and my family a distant second. As a young intern, I bought into the demands of the system to put my professional life above everything. As a result I missed out on many of the joys of parenting our first two children. Looking back, I now realize that I could have been both a good doctor and a good father without compromising either role. It's important that a child's main memory of his father is not one of seeing the father's back going out the door with a lunchbox or briefcase in hand. I want my children to feel that my professional career is very important to me, but that my fathering career gets top billing.

Dan, a new father who had a strong commitment to putting family before career, told me that he remembered his father being so involved in his work that even when he was home physically, his mind was still on the job. Dan had been so affected by his father's poor role modeling that he vowed not to repeat his father's mistakes. Sometimes modeling can have reverse effects.

You can also model your career satisfaction for your children. It helps my children accept and understand why I am away from home a lot if they get an occasional chance to see what I do when I am away. If possible, take your child with you to work and involve him or her in what you do there. I frequently take one of my older children with me on hospital rounds or to the emergency room to see a patient.

Father as a Model of Values

One modern viewpoint regarding the teaching of values is that parents should be neutral so that a child's mind remains open and he can decide for himself which value system he will follow. Not only does this rather simplistic method run contrary to experience and human nature; it can also have a disastrous outcome. A child who is a product of morally neutral parents will, at best, turn out to be morally neutral himself.

If you wait until your child is older to teach him about moral values, you are missing the period in his life when the ground is most fertile. When a child is older, he or she is influenced by many competing value systems. The best time to get down to the business of teaching values to your child is at a period when alternative role models are few. Three to six years of age is a prime time for receptiveness. At this age, a child readily accepts the values of his primary role models, his parents; your values are his values. Your child is still operating on the principle that what is important to you is important to him.

A father needs to use discipline and affection in order
to be an effective role model for his children.

After six years of age, most children are no longer completely receptive to their parents' values. They begin to be selective about which of their parents' values they will adopt and which values they will pick up from their peers. The older a child gets, the more he or she will question your values. A child matures by being exposed to alternative value systems and having to select which values will be incorporated into his own life. When parents lay a strong foundation of values for the child, he is less likely to be vulnerable to the onslaught of alternative values later on.

Father's role is to use discipline, affection, and his own consistent example to transfer his values to his child at an early age. He can then continually reinforce these values during those stages in a child's life when he is exposed to alternatives. The father's values become the standard by which all other values are measured. If the standard the child has been given is weak, then he is left to flounder in a sea of uncertainty, vulnerable to unhealthy alternatives.

Fathers may feel the weight of the world on their shoulders.

Father as a Model of Trust

Fathers are constantly bombarded with promotions for trust funds. "Plan for your child's future" is the advice of financial planners. Certainly fathers should plan financial security for their children, but money is only one side of the coin. Let me suggest another type of trust account for fathers.

Trust means that one person places confidence in another person for his own benefit. You will notice that trust involves two parties: the truster (the child) and the trustee (the father). Dad must first demonstrate that he can be trusted. Just as a financial institution spends millions of dollars to create a trustworthy image, dads must also demonstrate that they can be trusted—that they are strong, solid, dependable, respectable, and consistent. Financial institutions operate by creating the image that they can be trusted with your money. They spend millions of dollars on advertising to earn your trust. A similar trust can be developed by fathers but you first have to earn it, just like the big companies on Wall Street do. Throughout this book I have placed a great deal of emphasis on building up a trust with your child beginning when he is a newborn. Most presidents of major corporations in whom a great deal of trust is placed have begun at the bottom and worked their way up to the top. The growth of a father's image as being trustworthy is similar: start at the bottom (at birth) and work your way to the top as your child grows. That is how you build up a lasting trust account.

The child feels secure in the structure provided in the trust relationship with his father. Security is a major factor in child development. Feeling secure frees a child to be a child: to learn, to grow, and to practice his or her skills. Insecurity breeds underdevelopment. A child can waste so much energy worrying and floundering in an uncharted course that he wastes energy he could use to grow and develop. By providing trust, a father builds the framework in which a child can comfortably operate.

A trust account between father and child is indeed a long term investment. One of the commodities fathers have a shortage of is time. I once attended a seminar on time-management. The speaker advised dividing responsibilities and obligations into four categories:

1) High priority—high yield

2) Low priority—high yield

3) High priority—low yield

4) Low priority—low yield.

After the seminar, I said to the speaker "Jim, you just described fathering—if you give it a high priority, you're going to get a high yield." Many fathers waste so much time chasing dreams that seem to have high priority at the time but usually have low yield. I cannot imagine a responsibility which has a higher priority and higher yield than building a trust relationship between father and child. In terms of economy and capital gains, contributing to the father-child trust account is a wise investment.

Developing Sexual Identity

Fathers affect a child's attitudes toward sexuality more than mothers do (Lamb 1981). Sexuality means more than just sex. It includes not only the physical characteristics and changes of the developing child, but also the feelings and attitudes associated with these physical qualities. There has been more research on fathers' effects on the development of sexual identity than on any other aspect of paternal influence. The following discussion is based on the findings of reputable researchers as well as my own experience and opinions.

The Development of Masculinity

"I don't want my son to grow up to be a pansy," exclaimed John, a new father. His sentiments are shared by most men. What factors influence a boy's developing masculinity?

First, let me define what I mean by masculine. I do not mean aggressive, punitive, overbearing, domineering, bossy, violent, and loud. Instead, masculine means being assertive, decisive, responsible, logical, and able to take charge in difficult situations. These fundamental qualities should be founded on a basis of nurturance, tenderness, and ability to love and give.

Masculine attitudes complement feminine attitudes. For better or for worse, I believe in *"vive la difference."* Although sex role differences are not as clearly defined in today's families, I believe that differences between mothers and fathers are necessary for healthy sex role modeling. The healthiest sex role identification is found among children whose fathers clearly represent a healthy masculine role and whose mothers reflect a healthy feminine one.

The quality of fathering a boy receives is the most crucial factor in how he views himself as a male. A boy's masculinity correlates highly with the degree to which his father is available and behaves in a masculine manner in his interactions with the family. How your son perceives your masculinity is more important than how masculine you feel yourself to be. Studies have shown an important correlation between a child's perception of his father as a decision-maker, limit-setter, and disciplinarian and the development of strong masculine behavior in a boy.

I find it very important that sex role studies indicate that the effect of paternal masculinity on a son's masculine development is greatest when the father is also perceived as a nurturing person. These studies have dispelled the myth that a nurturing father may create an effeminate boy, a "pansy." Our traditional view that maternal nurturing is the prime determinant of a child's emotional and social adjustment may be incomplete. The father's qualities play an equal if not more influential role. Paternal nurturance is positively related to a boy's (and a girl's) success in peer relationships, cognitive abilities, and successful vocational adjustments. Masculinity without nurturing qualities makes a weak role model. In fact, some studies show a negative effect: a very masculine father who is not affectionate and encouraging may promote non-masculine behavior in his son. Perhaps the son who does not want to imitate his father's lack of nurturing behavior withdraws from imitating any of his father's other behavior, especially his masculine traits. Machismo without tenderness makes for an ineffective role model.

Father's participation in what are felt to be traditionally female activities (cooking, housework) does not affect a boy's masculinity. (Sorry dads, but research just doesn't support our lazy inclinations.) Doing housework is not hazardous to your child's sexual identity—or yours! The stereotype of the masculine, hard-working father whose only roles are breadwinner and child-punisher but who otherwise lies passively on a couch watching television, emotionally isolated from the rest of the family, is not a healthy model for children to witness.

Studies also show that if a father consistently adopts a passive role in discipline and family decision-making, the son is more likely to be low in masculinity. Be sensitive to how your child perceives husband-wife disagreements during decision-making. A child should not feel that there is a winner or loser. A child should feel that you respect your wife's input and that major decisions are made together, although dad may have the final say. This is especially important when the child wants a certain privilege and tries to play one parent against the other to obtain his goal. If a child does not know who is the final decision-maker, he is often confused.

I have a reason for stressing a high level of father involvement at home as an important part of sexual role modeling. I have long observed that mothers are more flexible and adaptable in child-care roles than are fathers. Fathers often have difficulty assuming the traditionally maternal tasks of child-tending and housework. Mothers are much more capable of taking over father's role if father is unavailable. Mothers seem to sense that a child needs the total package: nurturing and limit-setting. One without the other does not provide a healthy balance for an impressionable child. If father does not provide structure and discipline in the home, mother will. Mothers can become "masculine" more easily than fathers can become "feminine." While assertiveness in mothers and girls is as important a quality as tenderness is in fathers and boys, balance is necessary for healthy role modeling. One of the beneficial effects of the women's movement has been that today's mothers demand—rightfully—a higher degree of involvement in child-care from fathers. When dad does not make this investment in the family, mother must take up the slack and become both the mother and the father, a confusing model for the child. An available father can be more responsive to his son, thus reinforcing the child's approaches and encouraging him to reach out to his father more often. An involved and nurturing father provides more opportunities for his son to imitate his masculine behavior.

A mismatch of interests and abilities between father and son increases the risk of the child developing an unhealthy sex role identification. For example, an intellectual father with a son who has few intellectual interests or a sports-minded father with a son who possesses little athletic ability are both high-risk situations. The son may feel that he is not valued because he does not measure up to dad's interests and abilities. As a defense, the child may tune out this part of his father's personality and may eventually tune dad out entirely. Let your child know that you value him for what he is, not how he performs in a given area.

The Development of Femininity

Research suggests that father may play an even more important role than mother in a daughter's development of sexual identity. Fathers are powerful reinforcers of their children's behavior. A child learns to repeat those behaviors that parents reward and to shy away from behaviors that go unrewarded. Fathers, consciously or unconsciously, reinforce sexual development in their daughters. A father may, without thinking, encourage his daughter to participate in less aggressive, less competitive activities like drama, ballet, music, or cheerleading rather than encouraging her to take an active part in sports herself.

I have been guilty of this. I love ballet, and even before becoming a father I told my wife that if we had a daughter I wanted her to be a ballerina. Because of my encouragement, our eight-year-old daughter, Hayden, enrolled in ballet classes. It didn't last; after a few months Hayden decided to give up ballet for softball.

Fathers may not always consciously realize that they are reinforcing feminine personality traits. What is important is how your daughter thinks that you perceive her. Fathers tend to engage more in rough and tumble physical play with sons and in cuddling, nesting types of activities with daughters.

A father's nurturing behavior influences the
development of his daughter's femininity.

The gentler way you play with your daughter tells her that you regard her as sensitive and delicate and that she had better be sensitive and delicate.

Fathers tend to punish girls and boys differently, using more corporal punishment on boys. Could this be a way of reinforcing aggression in boys while encouraging delicacy in girls? Fathers are often more tolerant of academic under-achievement in girls than in boys. Another true confession: Upon receiving the news from school that our daughter Hayden may have a reading disability, my first thought was, "That shouldn't bother her too much since she may not even go to college." I would have been immediately concerned had this learning disability appeared in one of our boys! I soon realized that Hayden's future career plans may very well require a college degree, so we got her the extra help she needed.

Fathers are often more accepting of a boy with a difficult temperament than they are of the same trait in a girl. Disruptive behavior from a son may be excused with "Oh, he's just being a boy!" whereas the same behavior in a girl would not be acceptable.

Other fathers may have wanted a son instead of a daughter. They may never have "forgiven" the girl for not being a boy and may reinforce "boy" activities, showing satisfaction with tomboy behavior and discontent with more traditionally feminine pursuits.

A father's nurturing behavior influences the development of a daughter's femininity just as it influences a son's masculinity. Studies show that girls who are raised in a home where the mother dominates and father is passive, uninvolved in decision-making, and non-nurturing are more likely to have difficulty relating to and being liked by males later on.

How father treats mother also affects the daughter's femininity. If a man is involved, loving, supportive, and rewarding of his wife's mothering, the daughter not only has a healthier definition of maleness and fatherhood, but she also has a higher regard for the value of her own femininity. Your daughter may learn to value motherhood the way she perceives that you value it.

Cultural Stereotypes

I find it difficult to define masculinity and femininity without succumbing to cultural stereotyping. The term masculine often means assertive, decisive, physical, deliberate, logical; femininity is often associated with sensitivity, warmth, expressiveness, and ego-building qualities (used on the male, of course!). Perhaps it is more accurate to state that one set of traits predominates in a healthy masculine or feminine identity, but that each sex possesses some or all of the qualities in both categories.

Fathers are usually more influenced by cultural stereotypes of sex roles than are mothers. Fathers in general seem more concerned about masculinity and femininity than mothers. Mothers seem more able to encourage healthy nonsexist attitudes than fathers. One of my main desires for my children is for them to develop healthy sex role identities. I would frequently boast, "I'm glad our boys are real boys, and our girls are real girls." One day, Martha (who is more accepting of variations in sex roles than I am) asked, "Why is that so important to you?"

I'm beginning to realize that Martha's and my differences in regard to the importance of sex roles provide a healthy balance for our children. One parent constructs the framework for sexual development, and the other elaborates by conveying permission to the child to adapt some qualities associated with the opposite sex.

Fathers are known for their devotion to sex-role toys, whereas mothers are often less restrictive. A father gives a boy a football expecting him to kick it. He gives a daughter a doll expecting her to cuddle it. When the son cuddles the football and the daughter kicks the doll, father's well-laid plans go astray. Mothers, on the other hand, may give dolls to either boys or girls. I remember seeing our son Peter playing with a doll when he was two years old. My immediate reaction was to substitute a football, but the wisdom of my wife saved the doll for Peter. Healthier sex-role attitudes are developed when fathers encourage tenderness in boys.

Some Thoughts on Homosexuality

I want to say right at the outset that in most cases parents do not cause homosexuality. However, fathers should be aware that studies show that in some cases the sex-role functioning of the parents may increase the risk of a child becoming homosexual. And here again, father's role may be more important than mother's.

Inadequate fathering seems to be more of a contributing factor to homosexuality in both boys and girls than inadequate mothering. Boys who have ineffectual or absent fathers and close, restrictive relationships with their mothers seem particularly prone to homosexuality. I feel it is less healthy for a child to have a present but ineffective father than to lose a father through death or divorce. In the first situation, the father's role modeling will either confuse the child or cause him or her to withdraw from any relationship with the father or anyone else perceived to be like him. The child makes a judgment about the role model and reacts accordingly. In the latter case, the child whose father is not present because of death or divorce is at least free to search out or imagine what a father model should be.

Male homosexuals often say that they identified more strongly with their mothers than with their fathers. This is especially true of homosexuals who take a passive feminine role in their relationships with other homosexuals. Studies have also found that homosexuality is particularly common in families where there is not only the combination of a weak, uninvolved father and a dominant mother, but also a weak husband-wife relationship. The highest risk situation seems to be when a boy has poor models for all three family relationships: father-son, mother-son, and husband-wife.

Fathers also may contribute to a higher risk of homosexuality in their daughters. Interaction with a masculine and nurturing father provides a girl with a standard by which she can gauge subsequent relationships with males. As with male homosexuality, the quality of the husband-wife relationship figures in the development of female homosexuality. Poor father-daughter and husband-wife relationships may be particularly disturbing to girls. The girl has an unhealthy model for how fathers relate to daughters, husbands to wives, and men to women in general.

Some boys are thought to be at risk for becoming homosexuals because of their temperaments, interests, and physical characteristics. Fathers' reactions can increase or decrease the risk in these boys. If a boy does not live up to his father's image of masculinity, father and son may not know how to relate to each other. An important principle of behavior modification applies here. You must first meet your child where he is before you can carry him to where you want him to be. Many fathers become over-zealous in their efforts to "toughen up the kid" or they withdraw from their child entirely because they are embarrassed and disappointed. The son, in turn, may resist dad's attempts to make him into a "macho man" and may disassociate himself even more from traditionally masculine behavior. The healthiest home environment is one in which father behaves as a strongly nurturing and masculine person toward his child and toward the mother, and the mother behaves as a naturally feminine person toward both father and child.

I am personally concerned that our society tends to approve of lifestyles such as homosexuality. Society sees this as an "acceptable alternative." I can accept a person as a homosexual without having to approve of the morality of homosexuality. Keep the difference between acceptance and approval in mind when you consider the question of homosexuality as it applies to society in general and in relationship to your own family.

Modeling the Marriage Relationship

Most women who are satisfied in their marriages experienced a nurturing, affectionate relationship with their fathers and perceive their husbands to be similar to their fathers. Un-happy marriages and divorce are more likely among women who had poor relationships with their fathers. Sexual fulfill-ment is also reported to be lower in married women who had weak father models. Marriages are at an increased risk if husbands had inadequate fathering and consequently are unable to show and receive affection. As one mother in my practice confided "I'm tired of trying to do the job my hus-band's father should have done."

Fathers who take the attitude that the role of a man is to be a breadwinner and the role of a woman is to be a baby-tender will find that their children also come to believe in these rigid and unrealistic role definitions. While I believe that there are biologically determined primary roles for men and women in the family, I also believe that there should be a healthy amount of crossover. Fathers need to realize that such rigidly defined male/female roles may be imprac-tical for many of today's families. Also, adhering to narrow ideas of sex role behavior may deprive boys of opportuni-ties to learn tenderness with children while preventing girls from developing assertiveness and a sense of achievement. Over the past century, men's expectations of women have changed little, but women's expectations of men have changed greatly. Women expect men to take a more active role in child care (and rightly so).

Fathers can influence whether their daughters marry hap-pily and settle comfortably into the traditional role of at-home mother. Daughters who report a satisfactory relationship with their fathers are less likely to seek careers outside the home. Daughters of mothers who were happily fulfilled at home are themselves likely to become full-time mothers. A daugh-ter's perception of the value her father places on her mother's career also affects her career choice. If the daughter perceives that her father holds the full-time mother in high regard, the daughter is more likely to pursue the same career. Women who were successful both in their heterosexual relationships and in their professional endeavors tend to have fathers who encouraged their creative and intellectual pursuits without being heavily oriented towards sex-role career stereotypes.

For fathers who hope that their sons and daughters will grow up to enjoy marriage and family life, take heart. You can be an important influence on this happy outcome by being involved with your children while they are young.

Reference

Lamb, M.E., ed. *The Role of the Father in Child Development,* New York: Wiley, 1981.

CHAPTER 13

Fathering the Older Child

During the first year of fathering, fathers learn how to nurture their babies and build up their own sensitivity. Developing these qualities makes it easier and more fun to father the older child. Discipline is more effective when founded on nurture; play is more fun when accompanied by sensitivity.

Fathering the One- to Three-Year-Old

Toddlers learn by exploring. Parents need to have realistic expectations for toddlers' behavior. The child between one and three is impulsive, driven by an intense curiosity, and tends to get into everything. The parents' job is to channel toddlers' impulses into desirable, productive behavior.

The one- to three-year-old is going through interesting stages of development. He is mastering expressive language. He is gaining an increased awareness of himself—who he is and what he can do with the abilities he has. His motor skills are surging ahead. The child's ability to walk and talk makes it possible for him to express what he wants or needs and makes play and communication more fun for fathers. Most fathers really like this stage because the child can finally *do* something—like play ball.

Designing the Environment

Fathers can play a major role in channeling these abilities into the right directions. One of father's roles is to design an environment for the child in which he can satisfy his curiosity without damaging property or being tempted into undesirable behavior. This job should not be left only to mother. It is healthy modeling for your child to see you taking part and even being in charge of the home environment. Here are some suggestions.

Believe it or not, the young child's developing brain likes organization. The late Dr. Maria Montessori, founder of the Montessori method of education, in her years of observing young children noticed that they appreciate order. Instead of throwing toys haphazardly into a toy box, design shelves with one-foot-square compartments that will each hold one or two toys. (By the time their children are three, most dads are qualified to receive an honorary degree in shelf-building.) Making the shelves adjustable allows the height to increase as your child gets taller.

A row of wooden pegs at eye-level will encourage children to take responsibility for hanging up their clothes.

The greater number of positive memories the child has, the healthier his emotional development will be.

Children can learn to do this by three years of age. Buy or make child-size furniture. Having his own table and chairs in just the right size tells the child that he is important.

Build Positive Memories

Fathers can contribute to the emotional and mental development of their child through what I call the **input theory**. This theory is not something that has been proven, it's just my observation. Every parent-child interaction requires the child to attempt to perceive what the parent is communicating, make a judgment about the parent's intentions, and then respond with some reaction. This stimulus-response sequence is then stored in your child's mental computer like bytes of information. Later on when the child is presented with a similar stimulus he can automatically retrieve the patterned response that has been imprinted in his mind. Much of this retrieval information is stored either consciously or subconsciously in his memory. Fathers can greatly affect, for better or for worse, what is stored in a child's retrieval system.

For example, a two-year-old falls and scrapes her knee. Father, because he is present and tuned in, immediately comforts the distressed child. This interaction is stored in the child's memory as "I hurt—dad comforts." I believe that the early memories are stored in general patterns such as recalling only that distress was followed by comfort. In later development, a child stores more specific memory patterns such as how the distress is comforted, for example: "My father picked me up and held me until I stopped hurting. I felt so good." I would call this a positive memory input. A negative memory input would be, "I hurt and my father didn't pick me up." This negative memory is then stored in the general pattern of, "My father is not a nurturing person."

Another part of this input theory is the greater the number of positive memory inputs the healthier the emotional development of the child. If the child grows up with a predominance of positive and nurturing inputs, he or she operates from a basis of trust, joy, and spontaneity. On the other hand, if a child grows up with a predominance of negative inputs, he operates from a basis of mistrust, anger, and confusion. He is less responsive or more restrained and less spontaneous. In counseling, I have heard adults describe their responses to their children as being like "Playing a tape." John, a father of a very high need and difficult-to-discipline child, related that he often lost his cool and punished his child out of anger and both he and his child felt wrong about it. He related, "It seemed as though I was simply playing an old tape that is part of me." In going back into his childhood, John was disciplined by his father more from the basis of anger than the basis of nurturance.

Dads, while it is true that you cannot completely control the kind of person your child will become, it is awesome to realize that you can affect, positively or negatively, the memories that are stored in your child's developing mind. How beautiful if your child can later say to you, "Dad, thanks for the memories."

Feed Your Child Right
Fathers and grandparents are notorious for offering their children junk food. In many households mothers are more nutrition conscious than dads, and children are often confused by the mixed messages. By junk food, I mean foods like candies, desserts, and beverages that contain lots of sugar, artificial colors, and little nutritional value.

Some children are more vulnerable than others to the behavioral effects of junk food. A child needs a certain level of sugar in his blood for fuel for his muscles and brain.

Carbohydrates (sugars and starches) are your child's main source of fuel, but the wrong kinds of sugars (white cane sugar, brown sugar, table sugar, dextrose, corn syrup) provide energy in the wrong way. They enter the blood stream very quickly, causing blood sugar levels to be temporarily very high. This triggers the release of insulin, a hormone which regulates carbohydrate metabolism. The influx of insulin causes the blood sugar to plummet, and the child soon feels low, irritable, and hungry. A child's behavior often parallels his blood sugar, swinging from highs to lows. Healthy sugars (that is, fructose, found in most fruits and vegetables) and complex carbohydrates cause your child's blood sugar to be steadier, and this is reflected in steadier behavior.

Fathers often have unrealistic expectations of how toddlers and young children should eat. You can control what your child eats; to a lesser extent you can control when your child eats. You have very little control over how much he eats. Above all do not force a child to eat. You want to create healthy eating attitudes in your child.

Not only do young children lack the patience to sit still and eat three square meals a day, this pattern also may be unhealthy for them. A more realistic and healthier eating pattern is "grazing" or nibbling—small frequent meals throughout the day. A fun way to let children graze is to make a nibble tray, an ice cube tray or muffin tin with nutritious finger foods in each compartment. Getting young children to eat good foods requires some fancy marketing. Cut foods into interesting shapes to make them more appealing: orange wheels, broccoli trees, cheese blocks, melon balls, carrot sticks. Children should still be required to join the family at the table at meal times, but this can be thought of primarily as a time for family communication, not a time for force-feeding.

Sibling Rivalry
Sibling rivalry can be expected when children are close in age; it occurs less when they are spaced three years or more apart. While some degree of rivalry is to be expected, fathers can play a major role in minimizing this rivalry. Usually by

three years of age your child is used to taking all of mom's attention and she seems always able to give it. A new baby coming into the home pre-empts the older child's role as center of attention. It may be easier for this child to accept getting less of mom if he gets more time from dad. This is when a father can really shine with an older child. Doing special things with the child lets him feel that he, too, is special, just as the new baby is special.

Father's Role in Toilet Training

Fathers play an important role in helping toilet train their children, especially boys. When your son shows some indication that he is aware of body sensations telling him that he is about to urinate or have a bowel movement (squatting down, grunting, looking down at his diapers), that's the time to begin training. The two- to three-year-old has a natural desire to imitate, to do everything like dad. When you "go potty," encourage your son to imitate you in his own potty.

Father Fun

Playing architect.   The two-year-old is very creative and enjoys stacking, scribbling, building, and working with clay. Children between two and four (and older) love to build things with dad. One of our most memorable Christmases took place when I was still in pediatric training. We could not afford expensive toys for our children, who were then two and four. I went down to a local lumberyard and for two dollars I was able to fill the whole back of a station wagon with scraps of two by fours, four by fours, and other short pieces of wood. I brought them home, sanded them a bit, stacked them in interesting ways, and called them building blocks. Our children enjoyed and played with these blocks longer than most of the plastic gadgets they received on subsequent Christmas mornings.

Climb on pop.   Children love to rock on, walk over, and climb on, over, and underneath dad. They love to ride horsey, play bridge, do flips, and engage in a whole barrage of father-child gymnastics. Although mothers can usually participate in these gymnastics, too, children seem to expect and prefer father's roughhousing.

Reading and verbal games.   Between two and three years your child will show great strides in speech development. Even though your two-year-old may not actually say many intelligible words (called expressive speech), he probably understands most of what you say (receptive speech). In most children receptive speech matures much faster than expressive speech. Read to your child as much as possible, but in a meaningful way. Talk about the pictures in a book and associate them with the child's real world; while reading about the tree in the book point to the tree in the yard. The egocentric two-year-old loves to read about his own body parts and point to them and to yours. Naming games are a fun way for father and child to learn about each other.

Fathering the Three- to Six-Year-Old

Most three-year-olds seem to have their act together. Now that your child's verbal skills have matured, he can express his feelings with words, so that tantrum-like behavior usually subsides. Historical writings suggest that in ancient times the third birthday marked the beginning of a rapid increase in father involvement. This was the age at which children were weaned from the mother and began a more formal education with the father. The period from three to six years of age is a time when children are very receptive to learning values. This is the last stage in your child's life when he will accept your values without questioning them. Teaching family values is one of the prime roles for father at this stage.

As you designed your child's play environment during the previous stage, your role widens during this stage to include designing your child's social environment. From three years of age onward, a child begins to associate with others outside of the family circle. Keep your finger on the pulse of your child's social relationships and as much as possible direct him into relationships with children whose behavior exemplifies your own family values.

This is especially true when it comes to aggressive behavior. Children at this impressionable age should not learn to fight their way through life, to be tough, or in modern lingo, "street smart." Teaching a child to be too tough at too young an age usually results in an unhealthy balance of too much aggression and not enough tenderness. I feel that a child's values and behaviors should be firmly established in the first six years and only then should he begin to broaden his horizons a bit. A child should not be exposed to violence and aggression (especially on television) at an age when he is not able to make value judgments about these behaviors. In the next stage of development, between six and twelve years, a child can usually begin to make these judgments. Some fathers may feel that they want their child to learn about "real life" at an early age thinking that this prepares him better for the real world. We do not and never will live in an ideal society, but I do feel that the young child should grow up knowing what the ideal is or should be. At a later age he will realize and be able to cope with the fact that not all ideals can be attained.

This stage is also time for a child to have a one-on-one social life with dad. Here's a tip for busy fathers: take your child out to breakfast one day a week before work. With my daughters I call this a "Daddy-daughter date." Children this age realize that dads are busy, so taking time out to do something with them really hits home. My children call these outings "something-special times." These one-on-one times are especially valuable in large families in which children's individual needs may get lost in all the activity. No matter how many discipline problems you may be having with your child, make these special times strictly for fun and communication.

Save the criticism and chastening for another time. My children and I have struck a deal that we only talk about fun things during these special times.

Children like to help daddy during this stage—with washing the car, planting the garden, cutting grass. Doing household tasks *with* dad is fun; doing them *alone* is work. There will come a time when you will need to delegate chores to your child. If you get your child accustomed to working with you at an early age, it will be easier to assign the work to him when he is older.

Teachable moments.   One of the difficulties fathers have in exercising their role as a teacher is that children are very mood dependent. Your child may not be in a receptive mood at the same time you are available to teach. This is one reason that the concept of "quality time," while having some validity, is not very realistic for the mood-dependent child. By spending a large quantity of quality time with your child, you can take advantage of spontaneous situations I call **teachable moments.** You may be walking along with your child in a woods and your child, pointing to a bird, says "Look daddy, there's a bird!" This is a teachable moment. Your child has given you the opener that he has noticed and is interested in a bird. Here's your chance to expand on the subject. You can talk about how birds fly, different kinds of birds, etc. Teachable moments capitalize on a basic principle of learning: a child will learn best when he has initiated the topic himself and expressed his interest.

Preschool Selection
I have noticed that dads who practice the attachment style of fathering take a more critical view of their child's schooling. The school should be an extension of the home, not a substitute for it. This is especially true in selecting a preschool. Defining the time for starting school at a younger and younger age is part of a general trend toward increased parent-child separation which I strongly oppose. I feel that preschools are one of the great oversell jobs in American

society. There may be some homes in which the child must attend preschool because parents are gone during the day or because the child needs the enriched environment of a preschool. However, dads, you should not feel that your child will be educationally deprived if he does not attend preschool. It would be unwise for a father to work longer hours just to earn money to pay for preschool. That time would be better spent with the child. There are children who enjoy and profit from preschool; some three- and four-year-olds enjoy the social contact. Take your cues from your child and from your total family situation. If you sincerely enjoy having your child at home, your child enjoys being at home, and you and your wife feel comfortable providing your child with learning experiences and exposure to other children, then you are wise to resist the urge to place your child in preschool. If you and your wife do decide to enroll your child in preschool, attend the events and conferences at the school with your wife and child. This conveys both to the school and to your child that you will play an active part in his education.

Fathering Your Child from Six to Ten

As children grow older, they are exposed to peer pressure and alternative value systems, so they become more selective about family values. For this reason, fathers' continued involvement is extremely important in order to reinforce those family values.

Sports for Kids

Remember the days when sports for kids were simple? All it took was a dad, a child, a ball, and a sand lot. It's no longer so simple. The sophistication of the adult world has hit sandlot sports. Sports for kids are more organized today. Your child's involvement has changed, and therefore, father's role has also changed.

Sports can bring out the best and the worst in a child and in a father. Reflect on your own childhood participation in sports. What did it do for you? I can remember my senior year in high school when I was captain of the football team; I still remember all the strokes for my self-esteem that went with this honor. I can also remember a teacher calling my parents in for a meeting and telling them, "Your son will never amount to anything. All he does is study his football plays during study period."

Involvement in organized sports can have positive effects on children, both boys and girls. It can improve balance, coordination, muscle strength, and body awareness. It develops social skills, team spirit, and organizational abilities while promoting quick decision-making, self-expression, self-discipline, goal-setting, and learning about one's own capabilities and weaknesses. Sports also build self-esteem, self-confidence, and leadership qualities.

An inappropriate sports experience can negatively affect a child. Remember that a child is valued and values himself in comparison with other children. The child measures his own worth according to how he thinks that others perceive him. Your child may bat .300 on the baseball team, but he may feel inadequate if everyone else is batting .400.

The value-by-comparison factor has tremendous implications on the father-child relationship in sports. Convey to your child that he or she has value to you because of who he is, not how he performs. Compliment your child on his accomplishments and skills in relation to himself and his own improvement, not in comparison to others. This balances the child's own tendency to compare himself to others.

Prepare your child for the sport in which he will participate. Don't throw your child into a sport without any preparation or skill development and expect the coach to do the whole job. This is unfair to everyone. A few months before your child enrolls in an organized sport, start practicing with him and helping him develop the basic skills he will need. It is devastating for a child to realize on the first day of practice that all the other children are better than he is, either because they've played the sport before or have been practicing with their fathers.

Becoming involved. During the writing of this book, I managed a Little Leaque baseball team on which our ten-year-old son, Peter, was a pitcher and shortstop. Being a coach gave me a lot of insight into my son. I learned about his abilites, his weaknesses, how he performed under pressure, and how his skills improved from the beginning of the season to the end. Peter also learned the same about me: my weaknesses, abilities, and my control (or lack of it) under pressure. Getting involved allows father and child to learn

Involvement in organized sports can have positive effects, especially if dad gets involved, too.

about each other in a social setting. Many dads may not have the time or ability to coach their child's team, but you can get involved in other ways. You don't have to be an expert in a sport to simply show up and watch. Let your child know that what he is doing is important to you because he is important to you.

Encouraging healthy attitudes. I have coached winning teams and losing teams. It is very hard to keep spirits up on a losing team. Children want to win, and I'm not convinced that the desire to win is all a reflection of parents' competitive attitudes. We live in a competitive society, and competition in organized sports for children will probably get more intense. Your child will be competing with others during all of his or her life—for scholarships, for jobs, for influence. But you have to help children achieve a healthy balance. Encourage your child to do his best. If he truly feels he has given the team his best efforts, then winning or losing becomes less critical. When your child comes home from a game the first question should be "Did you have fun?" Then, "Did you do your best?" Last comes "Did you win?" Steve Garvey, first baseman for the San Diego Padres, recently said, "It's more important to have great fun than to be great."

Get to know the coach. As your child grows, more and more people will influence his physical, emotional, and ethical development. Coaches rank high as significant people in your child's life. Don't turn your child over to the mercy of the team coach without having some input. If your child has certain problems, tell the coach about these special needs at the beginning of the season. I remember the mother of my center fielder, Jamie, coming up to me before the first practice and confiding in me that his father had just left home and that would explain why Jamie was often angry. Several parents came up to me before the season and let me know their position on the "win at all costs" philosophy. They said that they wanted their child to learn sportsmanship and enjoy playing on a team and they weren't concerned with winning every game. This took the pressure off me. Parents can and should influence the coach's attitudes. Coaches may think parents consider them failures if their teams don't win.

Expect the coaches to model your family values. One of my assistant coaches smoked during a game. Several fathers complained and rightly so. Coaches are a model for the children. You have a right and obligation to expect any person of significance to your child to model your family values.

Finding the right sport. The sport should fit the child. A sport well-suited for a child can bring out the best in him. A poor fit can bring out the worst. Some children have athletic bodies. Some children are more physical, some more cerebral, and some excel in both kinds of activities. Every child can and should excel in something. Periodically take inventory of how your child is doing on the team. Is participating in that particular sport contributing first of all to his self-esteem and secondly to his skill development? A leading question may be, "Peter, how do you feel about playing baseball?" Encourage a child to become involved in a sport that he or she wants to, according to his or her own preferences and abilities. This choice may be different than yours. It is vitally important for a child to succeed, even if the success is slow and gradual. If a child doesn't fit the sport and continues not to fit, help him choose other activities in which he will be successful. Avoid making hasty decisions about pulling a child out of a sport. Children show a wide range of maturity at any given age. I have seen a "klutz" at the beginning of the season become well-coordinated by the end. Keep your finger on the pulse of your child's participation and wait for his skills to mature.

Some children who are doing poorly academically may have their self-esteem boosted by success in sports. Success in one field carries over to another. Oftentimes sports success will stimulate academic success and vice versa.

Sports are for girls, too! Gone are the days when organized sports were for boys only and girls were left to be passive observers. One of the healthiest changes in sports programs is the equal opportunity now offered to girls. Participation in organized sports helps to better prepare a child, son or daughter, for the future job market. Many of the leadership qualities necesssary in business management are similar to those used in team leadership. I once heard a management executive complain that one of the difficulties women have in upper management is with team leadership, a quality that they may have developed better had they participated more in organized team sports.

Fathers need to keep their eye on their daughter's sports activities even more than on their son's. There is a difference between assertion (demanding your rights without infringing upon someone else's) and aggression (infringing upon someone else's rights). Competitive sports should teach girls to be assertive but not aggressive in their relationships with others. I feel that aggression may defeminize a girl—but it is not healthy for boys, either.

Dad's taxi service. One of the problems of the modern father is not having enough time with his child. Taxiing your child and his teammates to and from games gives you extra time with your child. You can learn a lot about your child's level of self-esteem by noticing how he behaves in a car full of his contemporaries. This is valuable time, not wasted time. Take advantage of it.

Children Need Father's Approval
Dads, don't undervalue how much your child craves your approval. Our eleven-year-old son, Peter, brought this fact home to me recently. Peter was in a school play and I took my place in the audience as an admiring father. This happened to occur in the evening of a day that had been very stressful to me. I had several very sick patients in my practice and my thoughts were preoccupied with these babies during Peter's play. After the play, Peter seemed depressed and noncommunicative. I finally found out what was bugging him when he confessed, "Dad, when I looked at you in the audience you weren't watching me."

Dad as Business Consultant

A child's desire to earn money emerges during middle child-hood. Business ventures will not only teach your child about making money, they will also teach responsibility, mathematics, economics, and a few social graces. For example, our eight-year-old daughter, Hayden, and our eleven-year-old son, Peter, decided to set up a small produce stand on a busy corner near our home. I agreed to act as their "business consultant," but they would be responsible for operating the stand. They first had to decide how much to charge for the tomatoes and zucchini they planned to sell, so they went up to the neighborhood supermarket to find out the going rate for these items. Then they painted a sign and, along with their box of produce and a scale, set out on this enterprise. In order to make the situation more like a real store and to encourage them to use the math they had learned in school, I suggested they sell the tomatoes by the pound rather than the easy way, so much per tomato. I realized how much Peter had absorbed about the real world of advertising and commerce when he bribed his four-year-old sister, Erin, to sit next him, adorned in a pretty pink dress, in order to lure more customers to the stand. (How much fun it is to see children practicing what they learn from adults—for better or for worse.)

Peer Dependence

Between five and ten years of age, children's behavior and values are greatly affected by their peers. Because your child does not yet have the wisdom to tune out the values that run contrary to what you have taught him, it is necessary for fathers to keep tabs on what their children are learning from other children. This is especially true in our society where children begin school at an early age and are therefore more affected by their peers. The more your child is involved with other children, the more you need to get involved with your child. Reinforcement of family values is especially important during middle childhood so that your child enters adolescence firmly grounded in these family values.

A child who enters adolescence without strong values is easily confused and is more likely to adopt an undesirable value system.

The Middle Childhood Blues

Between the ages of seven and eleven, your child may have one- or two-week periods of seeming to be down. They mope around, appearing bored, tired, and somewhat depressed. Fearing that their child is sick, parents will often consult their

Independent business ventures can be useful learning experiences during the pre-teen years.

physicians about these blue periods. I feel that middle child-hood blues are similar to the mid-life crises that many men go through. This is a time when your child reflects on who he is, where he is going, what his friends think of him, and whether his parents really love him. Of course you love your child, but most important is what your child believes about the way that you and his friends perceive him. A number of factors contribute to middle childhood blues: dad being absent a lot, financial and marital pressures, sibling rivalry, school and social failure, and the child feeling that he is not succeeding in anything. A heavy dose of involved fathering is usually the best medicine for the doldrums. Schedule some special one-on-one times to have fun with your child and reassure him about how much he means to you. Fathering your child through these re-assessment periods can lay the groundwork for meaningful father-child communication dur-ing the coming adolescent years.

Father's Role during the Teenage Years

"My son is like an eagle. The nest is too small, and I can no longer hinder his flight." That's how one father described his relationship with his teenager. Nevertheless, fathers have an important impact on the turbulent adolescent years.

Guiding Your Teen

Adolescents are very active. They have enormous energy, often unbridled and undirected. Fathers can help channel this energy into meaningful activities that teenagers can han-dle. Adolescents sometimes overextend themselves with too many commitments. They often don't realize that they are in danger of burning out. A wise father can help the overex-tended teenager be more selective about his involvement in various activities.

Go with the flow. Teenagers vacillate between acting like children and acting like young adults; they're not completely comfortable with either role. Go along with your adolescent:

when he wants to be a child, support him as you would a child; when he wants to be an adult, respect this behavior, too.

Be approachable. If your teenager always gets a busy signal from you, he will quit calling. Even though much of his world lies beyond the walls of your home, your teenager must feel that the door is always open to him and that he can approach you for advice. Don't expect clear signals from an adolescent. He is unlikely to say, "Dad, I'd like to have your undivided attention for the next ten minutes." Many times during the writing of this book one of our teenagers would stop at my desk and ask, "How's it going, Dad?" If I gave him a one-word answer and kept on writing, the conversation would end right there. If, however, I looked him in the eye, shut down the word processor, turned, and put my feet up on the desk, meaningful conversation often followed. It was up to me to relay the message that I was willing to switch channels and give him some time.

Adolescents are impulsive. At a time when responsibility for the child's behavior is shifting from parental control to self control, unchecked impulses often lead teenagers down undesirable paths and into unwise decisions. The teenager must begin to take full responsibility for the consequences of his decisions and must struggle to make those decisions wisely. Here's where your early involvement with your child really pays off. If you have helped your child internalize your family value system by being an involved parent and by modeling the behavior you want him to follow, he will have the resources he needs to make wise decisions that will make you proud of him.

I explained this decision-making process to our oldest son, Jim, something like this: "Jim, life is a series of decisions. One of the things that I wish for you is that you develop the wisdom to make the right decisions. I believe that within every person there is an inner guidance system, something like the governor on the speedometer of our car—the buzzer goes off when we go too fast. This system can help you check your impulses when you are tempted to act without thinking about the consequences. If you aren't sure which path to take, make a 'pretend' decision and then live with it for a few days. If your inner guidance system continues to tell you that it was the right decision, then go ahead and make that your final decision. But if the buzzer goes off and you have a gut feeling that your decision wasn't right, then change it. If you develop your inner guidance system and heed its warnings, you won't go wrong. If you don't listen to those inner feelings, you'll desensitize yourself to your own wisdom, and you'll end up being indecisive or you'll make many wrong decisions."

From correction to counseling. During adolescence a father's disciplinary role shifts gradually from administering corrective measures to being a counselor. You're there to listen and react and guide, not to force your child to obey you just because you're the father. It is important that your child perceive you as a wise counselor, even if there are times when you may not feel so wise. You're still an authority figure to your child, but an adolescent has learned that authorities are not infallible. So listen carefully and explain your thoughts and feelings when you offer advice. This will increase the chances that your teenager will listen to and follow your guidance.

It's important that your child respect his mother's wisdom as well. It helps if dads point out that mothers are deeply intuitive about their children, and that even if they don't completely understand that intuition, they've grown to respect it. I've told our older sons always to be truthful and straightforward with their mother, because she can see right through them and won't hesitate to say so. It is healthy for children at all ages, especially adolescents, to feel that dad truly respects mom.

Privileges and Responsibilities
Another part of disciplining the teenager is handing out privileges and responsibilities in the right ratio. Keeping a

rein on your teenager means knowing when to let out and when to pull in. A teenager must appreciate the relationship between privileges and responsibility—with increasing privileges come increasing responsibilities, and only when the teenager shows he can handle the responsibilities does he get the increase in privileges. Teenagers are egocentric enough without their parents giving them a free ride when it comes to household and familial responsibilities. Being given responsibility is important to the development of self-discipline and self-guidance.

Car-key discipline. In some ways I find older teenagers easy to handle. I have something they want—the car keys. And the car keys have some strings attached to them. If my teenagers want the car keys from me, I have to see a certain kind of behavior from them. Some people might call this bribery. It is, and it works.

Influence, Not Control

When you're the father of teenagers, you have to face the fact that you cannot completely control their behavior. Most of their time is spent under the influence of people and institutions outside of the home: school, peers, church, television, entertainers, etc. You have to make an effort to keep in touch.

Here's a suggestion: at least once a month, take your teen out for some one-on-one time and really make an effort to talk about what's going on in his life. "Tell me about your new friend" is a fair question to ask. Don't worry that your teenager may think that you are being nosey. What he does is important to you because he is important to you. Most teenagers become increasingly private about their lives. However, in my years of counseling teenagers, I have heard more complaints about parents who are too little involved rather than too much. During these outings, provide a setting which allows your teenager to ventilate his feelings. One of the most common complaints teenagers share with me is, "My dad doesn't understand me. He doesn't even try."

These special times with your teenager are like taking inventory in your business. Just as in business, it's important to know where you stand with your child and where your child stands with himself. But don't go too far. A concerned mother once confided to me, "My husband tries to run our child like he runs his corporation. He tries to manipulate her and control her and seldom tries to understand her point of view." Children are not corporations. They have private lives that should be respected.

Adolescents need to feel loved. The issue is not whether fathers love their teenagers; it's whether the teenagers perceive that they are loved. Does your teenager feel that you love him or her? How many times in the past week have you put your hand on your child's shoulder, looked him or her in the eye, and said, "I love you"? Most fathers are surprised to realize that, in fact, they haven't come right out and used these words. Children never outgrow the need to be told they're loved. Don't assume that they know it; say so. Dr. Ross Campbell, in his excellent book *How to Really Love Your Teenager*, stresses three important modes for communicating your love: eye-to-eye contact, touch, and focused attention. Remind yourself to use all three of these communication methods daily.

Pay attention to how your child feels about himself. It is not too difficult to detect if your teenager is having a problem with self-esteem. Adolescents are not poker-faced. When they don't feel right, they don't act right. Unfortunately, much of an adolescent's feeling of self-worth comes from what he thinks others think about him. Parents have a right and a duty to monitor peer influence in regard to their child's values, but we can do little to influence whether a teenager's peers boost his self-esteem. The best thing you can do is to make your child feel that he is truly esteemed at home.

Parents must often struggle to avoid making a child feel that his worth is tied into his accomplishments. In many families, the mother is more concerned with the child's feelings, and the father devotes more concern to what the child accomplishes. Provided there is a proper balance, it may be healthy for mother and father to divide the parenting tasks this way. However, it's unhealthy for a child to perceive that his total worth in the eyes of his father is tied to his performance. It's true that, for better or for worse, much of a person's self-esteem is tied to his accomplishments, and it's naive to think that a child can feel great about himself but succeed little.

Our nineteen-year-old son, Jim, is currently struggling with his pre-med curriculum in college. I try to give him a dual message: that it's important to his future happiness and to his self-esteem that he develop his potential, but that what I most want for him is to be true to himself and to do his best. I will love him unconditionally, regardless of his success. The assurance of your unconditional love is one of the most important gifts you can give your adolescent.

Reference

Campbell, D. Ross, *How to Really Love Your Teenager.* Wheaton, Illinois: Scripture Books, 1977.

CHAPTER 14

A Closing Story

There once was a dad who got attached to his baby, and this is how the baby felt:

"Thanks, Dad, for being around when I needed you. I spent so much time with Mommy that you probably didn't even notice me looking at you. I think you felt left out at times, but I always knew you were there.

"Remember our birth. What a neat time! I felt as if I knew you even before I came out. I had looked forward to hearing you talk to me each night before I was born. I couldn't wait to meet you. When I slid out of mommy you were there, just like you promised you would be. You didn't have breasts or milk like Mommy, but I liked your voice and your touch, too. At first you were a bit scared to hold me. I could feel your arms shake a bit. We got to know each other right away. The way you carried me, sang to me, and snuggled me felt so good. After a while you got to be an old pro.

"Remember our first month together—the day I cried for two hours straight. I just couldn't get control of myself. Mommy was pretty upset, too. You wrapped me up and took me for a ride, and I felt better. Thanks for taking charge, Dad.

"Nighttime always scared me, but I felt so good when Mommy laid down with me the first night home. She knew the best place for me to sleep was right with you, and you agreed. I know I'm a noisy sleeper at times, and it was kind of hard on you. But you were always there to comfort me in the dark.

"Remember the time when I couldn't stop crying and Mommy was afraid I was getting too spoiled? I just wanted to be held, but I didn't have any way except crying to tell Mommy that. I felt so good when you told Mommy to stop listening to the lady next door and just pick me up when I cried.

"I loved falling asleep on your chest. It would go up and down and I could hear the thump-thump of your heartbeat while you patted me on the back. When you let out a deep breath I could feel the warm air from your nose on my head. And when you sang to me your whole neck vibrated against my head. That felt good.

"I remember your excited reaction whenever I did something new. That made me want to do it again. When I took my first steps, you were there. That was a big day for me, Dad, and I'm glad you were there.

"There were some days when you weren't so nice to be around. You seemed to be thinking about something else. Mommy would say that you probably had a bad day at the office. That bothered me. I wanted you to feel good, just like you always want me to feel good. I think that's called love. Sometimes you weren't too nice to Mommy, and that really bothered me because it bothered her. But you always made things right again. Thanks, Dad.

"I missed you when you were traveling, Dad. I could tell when you were gone. The whole house was tense, including

Mom and me. She was more fun to be with when you were around.

"Remember all the good times we had when Mom left us alone together? When I was tiny, it was kind of rough, and Mom wouldn't be gone very long because you didn't know what to do with me. But after a while we got used to each other, and we had more fun together. I still missed Mommy, but I really got to look forward to having you all to myself. Why do they call it baby-sitting? We never just sat around. You always thought of something fun to do.

"One day, after I had started crawling and could get around by myself, I saw this interesting cord hanging down from the table. So I decided to pull it. I didn't know it was connected to a lamp. Just as I started to grab it, you said 'No, stop.' Your voice wasn't angry, but it was loud and different than usual. I knew what you meant. You picked me up and took me across the room to where my toys were. They turned out to be more fun than a lamp cord anyway. Another time I tried to pull that lamp cord again. And the same thing happened. You rescued me again.

"Sometimes I don't trust myself, but I trust you. I don't always know what's right for me, but I know that you do. Thanks, Dad. When I grow up, I'm going to try to remember what it was like to be small so I'll know what babies need. Having you for a dad has helped me feel right."

THANKS FOR BEING MY DAD!

Index

Absent fathers, 4, 166-68
"Addicted" to baby, 6, 10, 57
Adolescents, 228
Advantages of breastfeeding, 51, 53-58
Alertness, stages of, 74
Ambivalent feelings, 22, 34, 35, 45
Analogies, 183
Apologies, 187
Attachment fathering, 5, 10, 13, 171, 237
and separation, 161, 170

Baby carriers, 79
Baby-sitting, 147, 237
Bad baby advice, 40, 41

Balance commitments, 159
Ball-playing, 108, 149, 224
Bedtime rituals, 116
Bending positions, 76, 78
Birth to three months, 68
Block play, 92, 105, 216
Body language, 84
Bonding, 10, 29, 35
Bottles, 65, 148
Burnout, 42, 142-45
Business consultant, 226
Body image, 46
Breastfeeding

advantages, 53-58
and sexuality, 123
at night, 114
father's role, 51
high need baby, 133

Campbell, D. Ross, 232
Career satisfaction, 2, 159, 196
Cesarean birth, 32
Changes in sexual behavior, 119
Chastening, 185-190
Childbirth classes, 19
Coaches, 223
Cognitive development, 103
Colic hold, 76
Communication,
 parent-newborn, 31
 regarding sexual needs, 126
Composition of milk, 52
Colostrum, 53
Comforter, 192
Conflict of wills, 176
Contingency play, 82
Continuous contact species, 53
Controlling
 feelings, 188
 impulses 184, 229
Corrective discipline, 185
Crawling, 95
Crisis situation, 195
Cultural stereotypes, 206

Decision-making, 194
Development, baby's first year,
 67-108
Diapering, 80
Discipline, 169-82,
 problems, 162

Emotions, 39, 194
Engrossment, 29
Expected behavior, 181

Family council, 181
Father hunger, 168
Father's role, 4, 6
 caring for mother, 33
 during pregnancy, 18
 giving approval, 225
 in breastfeeding relationship,
 51
 in childbirth, 25
 in making decisions, 20
 in setting limits, 178
 in teen years, 231
 with older child, 202
Fatigue, 120
Feeling "right," 37, 38, 237
Feeding tips, 100, 214
Femininity, 203
Foam cylinders, 93
Freeway fathering, 140

Games, 105, 150
Germ-fighting substances, 54
Getting involved, 4, 222
Giving, 36, 38
Greenberg, Dr. Martin, 30
Growth of dad, 6, 12, 24, 128,
 145
 of baby, 67-108
 older child, 211-33

Hand regard, 89
Healthier babies, 55
Hearing, 71
Hide the toy, 104
High need child, 4, 131-145
Holding patterns, 75
Homosexuality, 207
Hooked on fathering, 5
 on baby, 17, 33, 173
Hormones 6, 23, 42, 119, 123
 breastfeeding mother's, 57
 mother's, 57
Husband's sexual needs, 125

Influence on teenagers, 231
Input theory, 213
Investment in your child, 199

Juggling roles, 154
Junk foods, 214

Labor coach, 26, 28
La Leche League, 46, 244
Language games, 106
Laying on of hands, 7, 16, 17
Learning to walk, 102
Little nursing persons, 60

Mammals, 52
Marriage relationship, 18, 208
Masculinity, 200
Massage, 84-86
    bedtime, 118
Maturing as a father, 128
Middle childhood, 227
Mother-infant bond, 5, 10, 101,
    124
Moving toward dad, 101

Neck nestle, 76
"Nesting" period, 9, 19, 35, 39
Newborn, 30, 34
Nighttime fathering, 109-118
Nine to twelve months, 101
Nurturing ability of father, 50,
    152, 192

Obedience, 172
One- to three-year-old, 211
Orderly environment, 212
Organized sports, 221

Peer pressure, 226
Physical changes, 123
Pincer grasp, 97
Play circle, 95
Positive memories, 212, 213
Postpartum depression, 42, 49
Pregnancy, 7, 16, 22
Preschool, 219
Priorities, 196
Privileges, 230
Professional success, 2
Prolactin, 36, 155
Punishment, 169, 185
    girls vs. boys, 205

Reaching and grasping, 88
Reading games, 217
Reciprocity, 73
Releasing baby to dad, 10, 48
Respect for authority, 172
Responsibilities, 230
Responsiveness, 55, 57, 126
Role model, 191
Rolling and climbing, 93
Roll out the carpet, 108
Rules of the game, 180

Safety, 81, 151
Sailing incident, 195
Saying "no," 175
Self-esteem, 47, 183, 232
Sensitivity, 20, 26, 38, 41, 175,
    194
Setting limits, 178
Sexuality, 119
Sexual identity, 200
    role modeling, 201

Sexual needs, 23
  after childbirth, 122-25
  during pregnancy, 22
Sharing sleep, 112
Siblings, 40
  rivalry, 215
Sight, baby's, 53, 69, 87
Six to nine months, 94
Sleep, 109
  arrangements, 115
  cycles, 110
  disturbances, 112
Smiling, 83
Soccer game, 180
Spaceship story, 183
Special time together, 11, 30, 39,
  218, 231
Species-specific milk, 52
Spoiling baby, 172
Sports, 220
Starting solids, 99
Stereotypes, 30, 206
Super-sensitive baby, 132
Symptoms of burnout, 144

Take baby with you, 142, 173
Talking to baby, 72
Taxi service, 225
Teachable moments, 219
Teenage years, 228
Temper tantrums, 176
Third month, 85

Three to six months, 87
Three to six years, 217
Toddlers, 211
  normal behavior, 174
Toilet training, 216
Touch-time, 56
Toys for babies, 82
Traditional roles, 209
Tricycle in the street, 179
Trust, 171, 199
Tub tip, 75

Unborn baby, 15, 18
Unconditional love, 233
Understanding
  changes during pregnancy, 22
  high need babies, 134
  husband's sexual needs, 126
  postpartum mother, 39

Values, 196
Violence, on TV, 218
Vocal response, 73

Weaning, 58-65
Working from home, 165
  working mothers, 153

La Leche League's Growing Family Series

The books in the Growing Family Series are written to help parents know and enjoy their babies and children. Dr. William Sears, the series author, advocates attachment parenting, which focuses on the developing relationship between parent and child.

NIGHTTIME PARENTING
by William Sears
This book is for everyone: expectant parents, new parents, and parents of children with sleep problems. Dr. Sears, author of *Creative Parenting*, explains how babies sleep differently than adults, how sharing sleep can help the whole family sleep better, and how a particular style of nighttime parenting can lower the risk of Sudden Infant Death Syndrome. He also discusses night-waking, bedtimes, sleep disorders, and nighttime nursing. Mary White, one of La Leche League's founders, writes in the foreword, "This book will help all new parents raise happier and more secure children."
No. 276, softcover, 204 pages, $9.95

THE FUSSY BABY
by William Sears
You've fed, burped, walked, rocked, and cuddled your crying baby, but with no success—the crying won't stop. Your baby can't tell you what's wrong, and you've run out of ideas. How can you comfort your baby and preserve your sanity? This book has lots of suggestions, including "back to the womb" techniques and a guide to interpreting a baby's cries. Chapters on coping with colic, feeding, fathering, soothing, and avoiding maternal burnout include plenty of support and reassurance as well as day-to-day survival tips. "High need" babies demand extra patience from parents, but according to Dr. Sears, the extra effort pays off.
No. 289, paperback, 192 pages, $5.99

(Please include $4.25 shipping and handling for orders up to $19.99. In California and Illinois, add sales tax.)

La Leche League International
1400 N. Meacham Road
P.O. Box 4079
Schaumburg IL 60168.4079 USA
In Canada, send orders to LLLI Canadian Office
Williamsburg, Ontario K0C 2H0

LA LECHE LEAGUE MEMBERSHIP

As you read through the pages of this book, you'll notice several references to La Leche League. La Leche League was founded in 1956 by seven women who had learned about successful breastfeeding while nursing their own babies. They wanted to share this information with other mothers. Now over 9,000 League Leaders and 3,500 League Groups carry on that legacy. League Leaders are always willing to answer questions about breastfeeding and mothering and are available by phone for help with breastfeeding problems. League Groups meet monthly in communities all over the world to share breastfeeding information and mothering experiences.

When you join LLL, you participate in an international mother-to-mother helping network, a valuable resource for parenting help and support. Your annual membership fee of $30.00 brings you six bimonthly issues of NEW BEGINNINGS, a magazine filled with stories, hints, and inspiration from other breastfeeding families. Members receive our LLLI Catalogues by mail and they are entitled to a 10% discount on purchases from LLLI's wide variety of outstanding books and publications on breastfeeding, childbirth, nutrition, and parenting.

Why should you join La Leche League? Because you care—about your own family and about mothers and babies all over the world!

Return this form to La Leche League International.
P.O. Box 4079, Schaumburg IL 60168-4079 USA

_____ I'd like to join La Leche League International. Enclosed is my annual membership fee of $30.

_____ In addition, I am enclosing my tax-deductible donation of $ _____ to support the work of La Leche League.

_____ Please send me a copy of THE WOMANLY ART OF BREASTFEEDING, softcover, $14.95 plus $4.25 for shipping and handling. (In California and Illinois, please add sales tax.)

_____ Please send me La Leche League's FREE Catalogue.

_____ Please send me a FREE copy of the Directory of LLL Representatives. (Please enclose a self-addressed, stamped envelope.)

Name

Address

State/Province　　　　　_Zip/Postal Code_　　　　　_Country_

3/95